MIGRATION LETTERS

ISSN: 1741-8984
e-ISSN: 1741-8992

Abbreviated title: Migrat. Lett.

Migration Letters seeks to advance knowledge of human migrations and mobility by providing a forum for discussion of research, policies, and practices.

Migration Letters is indexed and abstracted in:

- Cabell's Directory of Educational Curriculum & Methods
- Cabell's Directory of Psychology & Psychiatry
- CEEOL
- China Academic Journals Database (CNKI Scholar)
- ERIH PLUS

- ESCI (Emerging Science Citation Index, Web of Science)
- International Bibliography of the Social Sciences (IBSS)
- Norwegian Register
- Research Papers in Economics (RePEc)
- SCOPUS

Migration Letters is published four times a year in January, April, July and October.

Migration Letters is published by Transnational Press London, UK.

Addresses:
URL: www.MigrationLetters.com
Email: editor@migrationletters.com

CREDITS: The logo by Gizem CAKIR and cover designs by Nihal YAZGAN.

MIGRATION LETTERS | ISSN: 1741-8984 e-ISSN: 1741-8992

MIGRATION LETTERS
An International Journal of Migration Studies

Volume 17
Number 4
July 2020

MIGRATION LETTERS | ISSN: 1741-8984 e-ISSN: 1741-8992

July 2020
Volume: 17, **No**: 4, pp. 477 – 485
ISSN: 1741-8984
e-ISSN: 1741-8992
www.migrationletters.com

MIGRATION
LETTERS

First Received: 6 May 2020
DOI: https://doi.org/10.33182/ml.v17i4.1085

Editorial:

Revisiting Borders and Boundaries: Exploring Migrant Inclusion and Exclusion from Intersectional Perspectives

Carolin Fischer[1], Christin Achermann[2], and Janine Dahinden[3]

Abstract

In recent years, scholarly interest in boundaries and boundary work, on the one hand, and borders and bordering, on the other, has flourished across disciplines. Notwithstanding the close relationship between the two concepts, "borders" and "boundaries" have largely been subject to separate scholarly debates or sometimes treated as synonymous. These trends point to an important lack of conceptual and analytical clarity as to what borders and boundaries are and are not, what distinguishes them from each other and how they relate to each other. This Special Issue tackles this conceptual gap by bringing the two fields of studies together: we argue that boundaries/boundary work and borders/bordering should be treated as interrelated rather than distinct phenomena. Boundaries produce similarities and differences that affect the enforcement, performance and materialisation of borders, which themselves contribute to the reproduction of boundaries. Borders and boundaries are entangled, but they promote different forms and experiences of inclusion and exclusion. In this introduction, we elaborate the two concepts separately before examining possible ways to link them theoretically. Finally, we argue that an intersectional perspective makes it possible to establish how the interplay of different social categories affects the articulations and repercussions of borders and boundaries. The contributions in this Special Issue address this issue from multiple perspectives that reflect a variety of disciplines and theoretical backgrounds and are informed by different case studies in Europe and beyond.

Keywords: *Borders and bordering; boundary work; intersectionality; migrant exclusion.*

Introduction

Much research on migration, mobility and citizenship revolves around instances of inclusion and exclusion. There is, however, growing concern that work on these areas of inquiry tends to rely on often unquestioned nation-state- and ethnicity-centred epistemologies (e.g. Anderson, 2019;

---

[1] Carolin Fischer, Ambizione Research Fellow, University of Bern, Institute of Social Anthropology, Lerchenweg 36, 3012 Bern, Switzerland. E-mail: carolin.fischer@anthro.unibe.ch.

[2] Christin Achermann, Professor for Migration, Law and Society, Laboratory for the Study of Social Processes and nccr – on the move, University of Neuchâtel, Switzerland. E-mail: christin.achermann@unine.ch.

[3] Janine Dahinden, Professor in Transnational Studies, Laboratory for the Study of Social Processes and nccr – on the move, University of Neuchâtel, Switzerland. E-mail: janine.dahinden@unine.ch.

Acknowledgements: This Special Issue was supported by a grant for a workshop by the nccr – on the move (National Center of Competence in Research – The Migration-Mobility Nexus), which is funded by the Swiss National Science Foundation [grant number 51NF40-142020]. This Special Issue is the outcome of the "Revisiting Borders and Boundaries: Gendered Politics and Experiences of Migrant Inclusion and Exclusion" interdisciplinary workshop that the authors organised at the University of Neuchâtel on 3-4 November 2016. We would like to thank all the participants for stimulating discussions and the nccr – on the move for having generously funded this workshop. We are also very grateful to Daniel Moure, who as always took care of the language editing, thus rendering our text more elegant.

Dahinden, 2016; Nieswand & Drotbohm, 2014; Wimmer & Schiller, 2002). In response to such criticism, this Special Issue collates novel approaches in the study of the dimensions, experiences, practices and politics of migrant inclusion and exclusion that combine theories of boundary work with insights from border studies.

In recent years, scholarly interest in boundaries and boundary work, on the one hand, and borders and bordering, on the other, has flourished across disciplines. Notwithstanding the close relationship between the two concepts, borders and boundaries have largely been subject to separate scholarly debates. This points to an important lack of conceptual clarity on what borders and boundaries are and are not, what distinguishes them from each other and how they relate to each other. Fassin (2011) is one of the few scholars to have explicitly addressed the links between borders and boundaries, without however clarifying the distinctions between the two concepts (Fassin, 2020). Given the on-going salience of borders and boundaries in the literature and in different spheres of everyday life (Yuval-Davis, Wemyss, & Cassidy, 2019), there is a need for more thorough reflection on the conceptual and empirical underpinnings of the two phenomena.

Theories of boundary work (e.g. Barth, 1969; Lamont & Molnar, 2002; Wimmer, 2013) and contributions to border studies (e.g. Van Houtum, 2012; Wilson & Hastings, 2012b) both focus specifically on the processes, practices and experiences of inclusion and exclusion. Analyses of boundaries typically examine how difference and social or symbolic exclusion are socially produced and organised, by which actors and with what effects. Boundaries thus involve the creation, maintenance, institutionalisation and contestation of social differences and concomitant forms of inclusion and exclusion. Border studies, in contrast, is predominantly concerned with borders and bordering practices. In this field, borders are not understood as mere physical lines that can be seen on a map. Instead, scholars in this field explore how borders and bordered territories are produced, regulated, governed, circumvented, lived and shaped by power relations, thus producing particular forms of inclusion and exclusion (Kolossov, 2005; Wastl-Walter, 2011; Wilson & Hastings, 2012a). Work in this field includes research on migration control focusing on the territorial and political dimensions of – sometimes de-territorialised – borders that delimit sovereign jurisdictions and define how access to and presence in the national territory is regulated and practiced (e.g. Coleman, 2012; De Genova, 2017; Walters, 2006). It also encompasses a growing number of contributions that engage with borders as part of cognitive and affective processes (Casas-Cortes et al., 2015; Mezzadra & Neilson, 2012). While the concepts of borders/bordering, on the one hand, and boundaries/boundary work, on the other, are usually employed in distinct fields of inquiry, the contributions to this Special Issue demonstrate that they should be treated as interrelated rather than distinct phenomena. Boundaries produce similarities and differences that affect the enforcement, performance and materialisation of borders, which themselves contribute to the reproduction of boundaries.

The seven contributions to this Special Issue draw on empirical research conducted in various social fields and at different geographical sites. They all expand on recent calls for more reflexive analyses of the migration apparatus (Favell, 2014; Horvath, Amelina, & Peters, 2017) and conceive of inclusion and exclusion as relational concepts that describe how access to participation, resources and opportunities is granted or denied to certain persons or groups (Achermann, 2013; Ataç & Rosenberger, 2013). Drawing on borders and boundaries as conceptual entry points supports this reflexive stance. Both concepts revolve around forms of inclusion and exclusion that mostly result from a nation-state-centred logic and therefore support scholarly inquiry that goes beyond a normalising understanding of differences.

Introducing the key concepts and the relationship between them

Borders and bordering

In his anthropology of borders, Donnan (2015) argues that the term "border" tends to be used in many different ways – to allude, for example, to the social, cultural, territorial or political nature of borders. Given such a variety of uses and meanings, there is a need to define what we understand by "borders" and "bordering". In a very general sense, borders delimit sovereign territories and jurisdictions and function as sites of control over the movement of people, services and goods by a sovereign authority. The first essential characteristic of borders is that they are both political and territorial. While for Wilson and Donnan (2012a, p. 18) the nation-state remains "the central thread running through" border studies, others (Van Houtum, 2005) stress the need to acknowledge that borders are best conceived of as multi-scalar phenomena. A key feature of borders is that they denote authority over a certain territory. However, they may delineate different spatial entities that are formally politically governed, ranging, for example, from cities to supra-national institutions like the European Union. As Paasi (2011, p. 22) argues, "borders are everywhere". Second, borders are also essential to cognitive processes, since they allow for the establishment of both the taxonomies and the conceptual hierarchies that structure our thought (Mezzadra & Neilson, 2012, p. 65). In Balibar's (2009) terms, borders make a world rather than divide an already-made one. In any case, borders rely on ideas of fictive communities, symbolically and cognitively constructed, and political will to become reality (see also Anderson, 1983). As such, they drive objectification processes, meaning that the "power practices attached to a border […] construct a spatial effect and […] give a demarcation in space its meaning and influence" (Van Houtum, 2012, p. 412).

It is important not to restrict borders to the specific, geographically determined lines we see on maps. According to Parker and Vaughan-Williams (2012, p. 730), borders "increasingly form a continuum stretching from within states, through to the conventional 'flashpoints' at airports, ports, and territorial outer-edges, and beyond to 'pre-frontier' zones at the point of departure". It is not the borderline itself that is relevant or the main site of interest, but rather the infrastructure, regulations and practices related to the belief in the existence and the performativity of the border (see Green, 2010; Weber, 2019). This is what van Houtum et al. (2005) strive to capture when introducing the concept of "b/ordering" as a way to describe the interplay between social ordering and border-making. B/ordering underlines the processual nature of borders – the ways they are created, maintained, performed, internalised and externalised (see Parker & Vaughan-Williams, 2012). The concept conveys a sense of open-endedness. It invites us to study the continuous construction of borders, how they are objectified in everyday socio-political practices (Yuval-Davis, Wemyss, & Cassidy, 2018) and deeply engrained in socially constructed mindscapes, identities and meanings (Van Houtum, 2012) and how they produce differentiated forms of inclusion and exclusion.

Still, one of the primary purposes of the border in a physical and political sense is to control, filter and govern the cross-border movements of people and goods. Although the link to migration, as van Houtum (2012, p. 405) notes, "is not necessarily a self-evident characteristic of the border", national border posts are one of the physical and symbolic instances where the selection between wanted/belonging and unwanted/non belonging is re-produced and performed. While borders fix the nation-state in space and time, they also regulate human mobility by demonstrating control over access to national territories, a phenomenon that De Genova refers to as the "border spectacle" (De Genova, 2017).

Borders not only produce territorial and spatial differentiation, but are also decisive to physical presence in a specific, formally delineated territory. Territory matters for access to rights because most rights are still tied to a certain jurisdiction and authority, usually a state (Dauvergne, 2014). By virtue of their legal status, persons either count as members of or aliens to a territory. Citizenship is the most obvious example of a status that determines access to not only rights, but also resources and opportunities.

Borders thus play an important role in enabling or restricting human mobility, in defining legitimate and illegitimate residents of a national territory and in determining the rights those residents have vis-à-vis the state in question. However, upon arrival at a destination, if not earlier (see the contribution by Dahinden et al. in this volume), migrants confront not only legal borders, but also boundaries as markers of distinction between different – imagined – national and cultural identities.

Boundaries

The concept of "boundary" finds its origin in the work of Frederik Barth (1969), who insisted that ethnic groups must be understood as the outcome of self-definitions and external ascriptions. Barth was the first to introduce an interactional, dynamic and relational perspective on the formation of ethnic groups. A large group of scholars took up and developed Barth's initial advances in the study and theorisation of boundaries. There is widely shared agreement that boundaries, as social constructs, establish symbolic differences between classes, genders, races, religions and so on. They produce identifications based on these markers of classification. Boundaries thus separate people into groups that foster feelings of similarity, membership, belonging and exclusion (Lamont & Molnar, 2002).

In her critical reflections on the prevalence of nation-state-centred biases in migration studies, Dahinden (2016) offers a poignant summary of boundaries and boundary work. The former result from dynamics of internal and external categorisation, in which a broad range of actors – including nation-states, the media, political parties and actors in everyday life – may be involved. Depending on the context and the actors at play, categorisation can be symbolic or institutionalised. Either way, categorisation and its underpinnings are fundamental to inclusion and exclusion (Jenkins, 1997). The analysis of boundary work thus provides insights into how difference is socially organised and produced, be it between, for example, nation-states or groups within them (Pachucki, Pendergrass, & Lamont, 2007). Nation-states, in this sense, are paradigmatic for institutionalised forms of social closure through boundaries, whose criteria for membership and access are clearly defined (Bauböck & Rundell, 1998; Dahinden, 2014). The principles of national or ethnic boundary work and concomitant forms of belonging, solidarity and groupness can, therefore, be considered to result from social processes that are at the heart of social inclusion and exclusion.

Borders and boundaries: How do they relate to each other?

The above sections suggest that borders and boundaries are closely related to each other, because both create differences and order by means of categorisation and classification. Parker and Vaughan-Williams (2012, pp. 729-730) note that "Borders are intimately bound up with the identity-making activities of the nation-state and other forms of political community. The modern political subject is 'bordered' in the same way as the state of which s/he is a citizen and this marker is performed through identity cards, national insurance numbers and so on". Bordering has inclusionary or exclusionary effects in the sense that it results in people being granted or denied access, rights and entitlements to participate in different realms of society. For instance, migration involves a constant process of re-invention and (self-)definition of both migrants and the national societies they enter. Similarly, van Houtum and van Naerssen (2002, p. 134) hold that "making others through the territorial fixing of order [...] is intrinsically connected to our present image of borders". As they argue, others are both necessary for the creation of borders and the result of the creation of these borders. In other words, the territorial fixing of borders contributes to the making of others.

By being bordered, the modern political subject is also subjected to boundaries in the sense that they are categorised as a member of or an alien to the national community of citizens (Parker and Vaughan-Williams 2012, 729-30). Formal markers of belonging, like nationality or a passport, are closely related to other, informal markers of classification, including ethnicity, race, religion, culture, gender and class. These markers reinforce the view of national societies as ethnically, racially, religiously and culturally homogenous entities, but the interplay of borders and boundaries can be contradictory: while someone may be formally included in the national community via nationality, they may still experience exclusionary boundaries deriving from, for example, racialised ascriptions of difference (see e.g. Fischer in this volume).

While borders/bordering and boundaries/boundary work intersect and are mutually constitutive and performative, they are often conflated or used in ambivalent ways. One example of this blurred distinction between borders and boundaries is the concept of "everyday bordering" recently introduced by Yuval-Davis et al. (2019). They observe that we have entered a period in which bordering has come to play a much more central role in everyday life. However, they use "everyday" to refer to both territorial state borders and social or symbolic boundaries, and they treat borders and boundaries as synonymous. Similarly, Brambilla's concept of "Borderscapes" (Brambilla, 2015) exemplifies how the concept of "border" becomes fuzzy when it is stretched to cover too much ground. We argue that bordering and boundary work are not the same, and that conceptual clarity requires that we maintain and theorise the distinction between them. At the same time, however, it is crucial to specify the relationship between the two concepts.

The contributions to this Special Issue demonstrate that borders and boundaries should be treated as distinct but interrelated phenomena. Boundaries produce both similarities and differences, which in turn affect the enforcement, performance and materialisation of borders, which themselves contribute to the reproduction of boundaries.

In contrast to boundaries, borders are necessarily related to states, which are territorial (Brubaker, 1992). Yet, as indicated earlier, this does not imply that border control and enforcement are necessarily limited to the specific territory of a given state. All the practices that fall under border control and border regimes involve filtering and controlling who is present in the national territory and who is subject to the jurisdiction of a given state. Boundaries can be but are not necessarily related to states, political entities or a given territory. They are broader phenomena involving multiple social and cultural differences whose creation and reproduction result in the creation and reproduction of different groups. Thus, boundaries define nation-states as "associations of citizens" (Brubaker, 1992). But boundaries are not limited to the state and the citizenry.

This distinction is important because it reveals that these two processes and phenomena require specific terminology. At the same time, it is necessary to reflect on how specific relationships between borders and boundaries promote distinct forms and experiences of inclusion and exclusion.

Adopting an intersectional perspective for the study of borders and boundaries

Because people are differently situated in the societies and social hierarchies that are delineated by borders and structured by boundaries, the relationship between borders and boundaries affects different people in different ways. As a result, it is vital to account for the social positioning or situatedness of the social agents (Yuval-Davis, 2013) whose experiences, reasoning and action are shaped by and contribute to shaping the interplay of borders and boundaries. Although there is no automatic correlation between a person's social location and their standpoint (see e.g. Hill Collins & Bilge, 2016; Smith, 1990), knowledge and meaning are indicative of certain locations that themselves are embedded in particular systems of power (Yuval-Davis, 2006). An intersectional perspective is helpful in determining and explaining the characteristics and effects of such situatedness.

An intersectional perspective makes it possible to establish how the interplay of different social categories affects the articulations and repercussions of borders and boundaries as reflected, for example, in particular forms of social behaviour and the social positions someone is assigned or chooses to adopt. Race, class and gender constitute the classical triad of categories included in intersectional analyses (Crenshaw, 1994). More recent feminist scholarship has extended the list of categories that can contribute to shaping an individual's position in society (like sexuality, age, migration and so on) (Winkler & Degele, 2010). Amelina (2017) argues that an intersectional perspective highlights the interplay and mutual shaping of various types of boundaries. It, therefore, lends itself to analysing multiple systems of classification. By means of categorisation, specific categorical distinctions are transformed into unequal life opportunities (McCall, 2005).

Overview of contributions

Informed by case studies from Europe and beyond, the articles in this Special Issue focus on the effects of intersecting categories of difference and illuminate the links and discontinuities between borders and boundaries while reflecting a variety of disciplinary and theoretical backgrounds. The analyses here go beyond a nation-state-centred epistemology while taking the potential relevance or irrelevance of national ethnic and other categories into account. Individually and together, the contributions demonstrate how combining theories of boundary work with border studies enriches our understanding of the dimensions, experiences, practices and politics of migrant inclusion and exclusion.

The articles share several themes. The first is the importance of an intersectional analysis. In the first – theoretical – article, Amelina and Horvath argue that an intersectional regime perspective makes it possible to better understand the interrelations between borders, boundaries and inequalities in migration contexts. Their argument implies that already existing analyses of intersectional effects should be amended to also include a focus on the intersectional dynamics of political rationalities that give rise to boundaries and borders. Amelina and Horvath explain how migration has been securitised, economised and humanitarianised, and how these changes are related to boundaries and borders.

A second theme common to many of the articles collected here is a focus on gender and gender equality as boundary markers in the dynamics and politics of cross-border migration. Based on the narratives of two ethnic-Hungarian women, Eröss et al. demonstrate how cross-border labour migration in the post-socialist context reinforces and repositions gender roles and boundaries. They argue that male and female cross-border migration has accelerated various shifts in family life.

Focusing specifically on the interplay of gender and cross-border migration, the article reveals the ambivalences of gendered boundaries in the post-socialist context.

Dahinden et al. examine how European nation-states and the EU continuously reproduce themselves in a globalised world by producing particular outsiders. Through a case study of cross-border marriages among Tamil women in Sri Lanka, they demonstrate the co-constitutive nature of bordering practices and boundary making. Most European countries restrict cross-border marriages by simultaneously internalising and externalising their borders and by mobilising specific understandings of gender (in)equality as a symbolic boundary. By combining border and boundary perspectives, this article reveals new processes of exclusion and inclusion that reinforce global inequalities and postcolonial governmentalities.

Another pair of contributions examine how different – often racialised – boundaries are mobilised to legitimise one's own position in society or to question or retain social hierarchies or institutions in bounded national contexts. In her contribution, Rezzonico explores immigration detention in Switzerland. She examines how staff working at detention centres construct and reproduce boundaries by distancing themselves from detainees. This boundary work enables officers to remain aloof from the pain experienced by detainees, and to legitimise their role in an exclusionary institution. Through the construction of detainees as culturally and morally different, illegal and undeserving, as well as potentially dangerous, detention officers contribute to the reinforcement and legitimisation of borders.

To demonstrate how the effects of borders and boundaries coincide in people's everyday lives, Fischer examines the normative principle and politics of migrant integration. To this end, she explores how descendants of migrants in Zürich mobilise notions of integration to describe their experiences and sense of belonging or non-belonging to society. She demonstrates how persons who were born and raised in immigrant families experience, interpret, appropriate and modify their understanding of integration in regard to themselves and perceived others. These understandings of integration demonstrate how the interplay of borders and boundaries affects individual meaning-making, perceptions of self and other and the way people situate themselves in society.

Finally, several of the articles examine the role of emotions and affect in the construction of borders and boundaries, on the one hand, and in shaping individual experiences of borders and boundaries, on the other. Drawing on two cases from Austria, Scheibelhofer argues that a focus on emotion and affect improves our understanding of how borders and boundaries are constructed and negotiated. First, he demonstrates how the state used the politics of fear in the aftermath of the 2015 "refugee crisis" to re-impose control after a brief period during which it permitted relatively free movement. Second, in examining sponsorship relationships between volunteers and young male refugees, he unpacks the effects of pity, intimacy and solidarity in a context of complex power hierarchies. Scheibelhofer demonstrates that emotions can both contribute to maintaining boundaries and legitimating restrictive border politics and instigate transgressions of established boundaries between "us" and "them".

In her case study of Romanian citizens living in the United Kingdom, Cassidy examines how their experiences not only exemplify the intersection of borders and boundary work, but are also influenced by the ways in which they manage their emotions. Cassidy demonstrates how members of minoritised groups unconsciously perform border and boundary work. Her contribution also demonstrates how the complex entanglements of (re)bordering and socio-cultural boundaries are experienced by a specific migrant group.

With their variety of case studies, analytical entry points and theoretical perspectives, the contributions to this Special Issue make important advances in bringing together the study of borders and boundaries as prominent fields of inquiry in contemporary migration studies. Through the questions they raise, they also offer intriguing points of departure for future inquiry.

References

Achermann, C. (2013). Excluding the unwanted: dealing with foreign-national offenders in Switzerland. In I. Ataç & S. Rosenberger (Eds.), *Politik der Inklusion und Exklusion* (pp. 91-109). Göttingen: V&R unipress.

Amelina, A. (2017). *Transnationalizing Inequalities in Europe. Sociocultural Boundaries, Assemblages and Regimes of Intersection*. New York and London: Routledge.

Anderson, B. (1983). *Imagined Communities*. London: Verso.

Anderson, B. (2019). New Directions in Migration Studies: Towards Methodological Denationalism. *Comparative Migration Studies, 7*(1).

Ataç, I., & Rosenberger, S. (2013). Inklusion/Exklusion - ein relationales Konzept der Migrationsforschung. In I. Ataç & S. Rosenberger (Eds.), *Politik der Inklusion und Exklusion* (pp. 32-52). Göttingen: V&R unipress.

Balibar, E. (2009). Europe as Borderland. *Environment and Planning D: Society and Space, 27*(2), 190-215. doi:10.1068/d13008

Barth, F. (1969). Introduction. In F. Barth (Ed.), *Ethnic Groups and Boundaries: The Social Organization of Culture Difference* (pp. 9-38). London: Allen & Unwin.

Bauböck, R., & Rundell, J. (Eds.). (1998). *Blurred Boundaries: Migration, Ethnicity, Citizenship*. Aldersho: Ashgate Publishing Limited.

Brambilla, C. (2015). Exploring the Critical Potential of the Borderscapes Concept. *Geopolitics, 20*(1), 14-34. doi:10.1080/14650045.2014.884561

Brubaker, R. (1992). *Citizenship and Nationhood in France and Germany*. Cambridge, Mass.: Harvard University Press.

Casas-Cortes, M., Cobarrubias, S., De Genova, N., Garelli, G., Grappi, G., Heller, C., . . . Tazzioli, M. (2015). New Keywords: Migration and Borders. *Cultural Studies, 29*(1), 55-87. doi:10.1080/09502386.2014.891630

Coleman, M. (2012). From border policing to internal immigration control in the United States. In T. M. Wilson & H. Donnan (Eds.), *A Companion to Border Studies* (pp. 419-437). Hoboken: Wiley Blackwell.

Crenshaw, K. W. (1994). Mapping the Marigins: Intersectionality, Identity Politics, and Violence Against Women of Colour. In M. Albertson Fineman & R. Mykitiuk (Eds.), *The Public Nature of Private Violence* (pp. 92-118). New York: Routeledge.

Dahinden, J. (2014). "Kultur" als Form symbolischer Gewalt: Grenzziehungen im Kontext von Migration am Beispiel der Schweiz. In B. Nieswand & H. Drotbohm (Eds.), *Kultur, Gesellschaft, Migration: Die reflexive Wende in der Migrationsforschung* (pp. 97-122). Wiesbaden: VS/Springer.

Dahinden, J. (2016). A plea for the 'de-migranticization' of research on migration and integration. *Ethnic and Racial Studies, 39*(13), 2207-2225. doi:10.1080/01419870.2015.1124129

Dauvergne, C. (2014). Irregular Migration, State Souvereignity and the Rule of Law. In V. Chetail & C. Bauloz (Eds.), *Research Handbook on International Law and Migration* (pp. 75-92). Cheltenham: Edward Elgar Publishing.

De Genova, N. (2017). The Borders of "Europe" and the European Question. In N. De Genova (Ed.), *The Borders of "Europe": Autonomy of Migration, Tactics of Bordering* (pp. 1-35). Durham and London: Duke University Press.

Donnan, H. (2015). The Anthropology of Borders. In J. D. Wright (Ed.), *International Encyclopedia of the Social and Behavioral Sciences* (pp. 760-765). Oxford: Elsevier.

Fassin, D. (2011). Policing Borders, Producing Boundaries. The Governmentality of Immigration in Dark Times. *Annual Review of Anthropology, 40*(213-26).

Fassin, D., 2020. *Deepening divides : how territorial borders and social boundaries delineate our world, Anthropology, culture and society*. Pluto Press, London.

Favell, A. (2014). *Immigration, Integration and Mobility: New Agendas in Migration Studies. Essays 1998–2014*. Colchester: ECPR Press.

Green, S. (2010). Performing Border in the Aegean. *Journal of Cultural Economy, 3*(2), 261-278. doi:10.1080/17530350.2010.494376

Hill Collins, P., & Bilge, S. (2016). *Intersectionality*. Cambridge: Polity Press.

Horvath, K., Amelina, A., & Peters, K. (2017). Re-thinking the politics of migration. On the uses and challenges of regime perspectives for migration research. *Migration Studies, 5*(3), 301-314. doi:10.1093/migration/mnx055

Jenkins, R. (1997). *Rethinking Ethnicity: Arguments and Explorations*. London: Sage.

Kolossov, V. (2005). Border Studies: Changing Perspectives and Theoretical Approaches. *Geopolitics, 10*(4), 606-632.

Lamont, M., & Molnar, V. (2002). The Study of Boundaries in the Social Sciences. *Annual Review of Sociology, 28*, 167-195.

McCall, L. (2005). The complexity of intersectionality. *Journal of Women in Culture and Society, 30*(3), 1771-1800.

Mezzadra, S., & Neilson, B. (2012). Between Inclusion and Exclusion: On the Topology of Global Space and Borders. *Theory, Culture & Society, 29*(4/5), 58-78.

Nieswand, B., & Drotbohm, H. (2014). Einleitung: Die reflexive Wende in der Migrationsforschung. In B. Nieswand & H. Drotbohm (Eds.), *Kultur, Gesellschaft, Migration. Studien zur Migrations- und Integrationspolitik* (pp. 1-37): Springer.

Paasi, A. (2011). A Border Theory: An Unattainable Dream or a Realistic Aim for Border Scholars? In D. Wastl-Walter (Ed.), *The Ashagate Resaerch Campanion to Border Studies* (pp. 11-32). Farham: Ashate.

Pachucki, M. A., Pendergrass, S., & Lamont, M. (2007). Boundary Processes: Recent Theoretical Developments and New Contributions. *Poetics, 35*, 331-351.

Parker, N., & Vaughan-Williams, N. (2012). Critical Border Studies: Broadening and Deepening the 'Lines in the Sand' Agenda. *Geopolitics, 17*(4), 727-733. doi:10.1080/14650045.2012.706111

Smith, D. E. (1990). *The conceptual practices of power: a feminist sociogy of knowledge*. Boston: Northeastern University Press.

Van Houtum, H. (2005). The Geopolitics of Borders and Boundaries. *Geopolitics, 10*(4), 672-679. doi:10.1080/14650040500318522

Van Houtum, H. (2012). Remappng borders. In T. M. Wilson & H. Donnan (Eds.), *A Companion to Border Studies* (pp. 405-418). Hoboken: Wiley Blackwell.

Van Houtum, H., Kramsch, O. T., & Zierhofer, W. (2005). B/ordering space. In H. Van Houtum, O. T. Kramsch, & W. Zierhofer (Eds.), *B/ordering space* (Vol. 1-13). Ashgate: Aldershot.

Van Houtum, H., & Van Naerssen, T. (2002). Bordering, Ordering and Othering. *Tijdschrift voor economische en sociale geografie, 93*(2), 125-136. doi:10.1111/1467-9663.00189

Walters, W. (2006). Border/Control. *European Journal of Social Theory, 9*(2), 187-203. doi:10.1177/1368431006063332

Wastl-Walter, D. (2011). *The Ashgate Research Companion to Border Studies*. Farnham: Ashgate.

Weber, L. (2019). From state-centric to transversal borders: Resisting the 'structurally embedded border' in Australia. *Theoretical Criminology, 23*(2), 228-246. doi:10.1177/1362480618819795

Wilson, T. M., & Hastings, D. (2012a). Borders and Border Studies. In T. M. Wilson & D. Hastings (Eds.), *A companion to Border Studies* (pp. 1-25): Blackwell Publications Ltd.

Wilson, T. M., & Hastings, D. (Eds.). (2012b). *A Companion to Border Studies*: Blackwell Publishing Ltd.

Wimmer, A. (2013). *Ethnic Boundary Making. Institutions, Power and Networks*. Oxford: Oxford University Press.

Wimmer, A., & Schiller, N. G. (2002). Methodological Nationalism and Beyond: Nation-State Building, Migration and the Social Sciences. *Global Networks, 2*(4), 301-334.

Winkler, G., & Degele, N. (2010). *Intersektionalität. Zur Analyse sozialer Ungleichheiten*. Bielefeld: Transcript.

Yuval-Davis, N. (2006). Intersectionality and Feminist Politics. *European Journal of Women's Studies, 13*(193-203).

Yuval-Davis, N. (2013). A situated intersectional everyday approach to the study of bordering. *EU Borderscaptes Working Papers No. 2*.

Yuval-Davis, N., Wemyss, G., & Cassidy, K. (2018). Everyday Bordering, Belonging and the Reorientation of British Immigration Legislation. *Sociology, 52*(2), 228-244. doi:10.1177/0038038517702599

Yuval-Davis, N., Wemyss, G., & Cassidy, K. (2019). *Bordering*. Cambridge: Polity Press.

July 2020
Volume: 17, **No**: 4, pp. 487 – 497
ISSN: 1741-8984
e-ISSN: 1741-8992
www.migrationletters.com

MIGRATION
LETTERS

First Submitted: 20 February 2019 Accepted: 22 August 2019
DOI: https://doi.org/10.33182/ml.v17i4.710

Regimes of Intersection: Facing the Manifold Interplays of Discourses, Institutions, and Inequalities in the Regulation of Migration

Anna Amelina[1] and Kenneth Horvath[2]

Abstract

This article proposes to move towards an intersectional regime perspectives to enhance our understanding of the interrelations of borders, boundaries, and inequalities in migration contexts. It addresses a conspicuous mismatch in current research: While the contingencies and context-dependencies of migration regimes are widely acknowledged, little attention has been paid to the actual interwoven mechanisms and processes that link political orders to social formations. We suggest amending already existing analyses of intersectional effects of migration-related 'lines of oppression' in two regards. First, we argue for focusing on the intersectional dynamics of political rationalities that give rise to boundaries and borders (the securitisation, the economisation, and the humanitarianisation of migration). Second, we highlight the need to investigate the intersections between different fields of practice involved in the implementation and enactment of boundaries and borders. We conclude by identifying key challenges and promises of an intersectional regime perspective for migration research.

Keywords: *Migration regimes; inequalities; borders; boundaries; intersectionality.*

Introduction

Recent research emphasises the context-dependency, contingency, and conditionality of migration regimes[3] (Horvath et al., 2017). Migration regimes are complex social formations that entail an interplay among border, mobility, and citizenship regulations; they are shaped by and implemented through an interplay of various institutions and fields of practice, only few of which qualify as 'political' in a narrow sense; and their effects develop within contexts of interwoven class-related, gendered, and ethnicised/racialised structures of inequality. In short, migration regimes are marked by manifold intersectionalities.

The key argument of this article is that the tools for conceptualising and researching these intersectionalities need to be refined. We argue that there is a need to move from implicit presumptions to explicit theorisation about the manifold interplays involved in the political regulation of migration. An intersectional migration-regime theory would, among other things, enhance our understanding of the interplay of borders and boundaries. Borders, in our understanding, are political technologies or dispositifs that regulate entry, settlement and related citizenship rights; boundaries, in contrast, are knowledge forms – social classifications that are intimately linked to hierarchies and inequalities. One of the central objectives of an intersectional

---

[1] Anna Amelina, University of Cottbus, Germany. E-mail: anna.amelina@b-tu.de.
[2] Kenneth Horvath, University of Lucerne, Switzerland. E-mail: kenneth.horvath@unilu.ch.
[3] For reasons of readability and brevity, we use 'migration regime' in this article as a shorthand for the more accurate notion of 'border, boundary, citizenship, and mobility regimes'.

regime perspective is to decipher how borders and boundaries, thus understood, are entangled with current structures of inequality and dynamics of inclusion and exclusion.

Such an intersectional fine-tuning can, of course, build on existing feminist theories of intersectionality (Anthias, 2001; Walby, 2009; Lutz et al., 2011; Amelina, 2017). The main purpose of this paper is to substantiate our key argument that there, however, is a need to widen the scope of intersectionalities taken into account in two directions. Apart from the structural effects of interlocking lines of oppression (already addressed in existing studies), we, first, need to pay attention to the intersectional dynamics that give rise to borders and boundaries in the first place. More concretely, we argue for inquiring into the interplays between different political rationalities "such as economisation, securitisation and humanitarianization" that underpin the emergence and functioning of boundaries and borders. Second, we use the example of educational institutions to illustrate the need to investigate the manifold interplays of institutions and fields of practice involved in implementing and enacting boundaries and borders once they are established. We conclude by identifying the implications of an intersectional regime perspective for future empirical research.

Intersectional regime perspectives: Contours of an analytical program

Against the background of the recent massive politicisation of migration, regime perspectives have become rather prominent in migration research (Hammar, 2007; van der Brug et al., 2015; Pott et al., 2018). It should be noted that 'regime' is not a unified or solidified concept. Current understandings in migration research draw on different sources, including welfare state studies (Esping-Andersen, 1990; Sainsbury, 2006), the French regulation school (Boyer and Saillard, 2002; Mezzadra and Neilson, 2012), and Foucauldian governmentality studies (Walters, 2006; de Genova and Peutz, 2010). Nevertheless, these different regime theories converge in relevant ways (Horvath et al., 2017). Most importantly, they shift the focus from explicit wordings and presumed intentions of migration policies to the interplay of discourses, institutions, and practices involved in regulating borders and mobilities (Sciortino, 2004). This understanding is already expressed in Krasner's (1982) seminal definition of regimes as 'networks of rules, norms, and procedures that regularise behaviour and control its effects'.

Thus understood, regime concepts sensitise for the complexities, contingencies, and conditionalities of regulating and governing migration. They focus our attention on processes and relations and on how migration regimes develop their effects through an interplay with wider political and societal contexts. Consequently, regime perspectives in migration cannot restrict themselves to either one 'axis of difference' (such as legal status, citizenship, or ethnicity/race) or to one field of social practice (such as politics, understood in a narrow sense). They inherently require an 'intersectional' outlook, and the interplays of interest can take very different forms. For example, scholars have investigated the interdependencies of global and national scales in policy implementation (Bartels, 2017); the interlinked social, political, and administrative dynamics involved in refugee status determination (Dahlvik, 2018); the interplay between wider societal discourses and migrant-citizen subjectivities (Badenhoop, 2017); the links between local and national scales in determining the housing conditions of refugee populations (El-Kayed and Hamann, 2018); or the interrelations between labour market dynamics and legal classifications (Engbersen et al., 2017). For the most part, however, these various intersectional dynamics are discussed only implicitly (not surprisingly, notable exceptions focus on gender-related issues, e.g. Lutz, 2017 or Schwenken, 2018).

Our key argument is that we need to move from implicitly assuming to explicitly theorising and researching the intersectional dynamics of current border and migration politics. Such an intersectional regime perspective can build on classical feminist theories of intersectionality which have become quite visible in sociological analyses of inequalities (bell hooks, 1981; King, 1988; Collins, 2000; Anthias, 2001; Walby, 2009; Lutz et al., 2011). The core of this theoretical perspective (with its different variants) is that inequalities, understood as unequal distribution of life chances and life opportunities (cf. Anthias, 2001), are generated by an interplay of various types of 'oppressions', with gender, ethnicity/race, class, sexuality, health/disability, age/life course, and space being treated as the currently dominant 'axes of difference' (Becker-Schmidt, 2007; Walby, 2009; Amelina, 2017). This interplay has been approached as a 'multiple jeopardy' (King, 1988) or as an interlocking of systems of oppression (Collins, 2000).

Our reading of intersectional theory highlights the crucial role of knowledge orders for the generation, reproduction, and transformation of inequalities. 'Axes of difference' are forms of social classification that are interwoven with social inequalities. As such, they are discursive phenomena, forms of societal knowledge that are deeply anchored in and entangled with political formations, societal institutions, and everyday practices. Moving towards intersectional regime analysis requires to put a strong focus on this social, cultural, and political embedding of intersectional classifications. In addition to determining how some classifications (once established) interact with other patterns of inequality, we also need to consider the intersectional political dynamics that give rise to them and the concrete interplay of institutions and practices involved in their daily enactment.

The concepts of boundaries and boundary-making provide a viable anchor point for grasping comparable intersectional dynamics in current migration regimes (Lamont and Molnár, 2002; Wimmer, 2013; Amelina, 2017). Boundaries are social classifications – forms of knowledge – that are closely tied up with social hierarchies. They are 'made' in concrete practices in various social fields (such as journalism, the social sciences, state administration, or private businesses) (Fassin, 2011b). The making of (hierarchical) boundaries will, in many cases, not be explicit and intentional, but will rather follow unintentionally from professional classification and categorisation[4] practices (Horvath, 2019). The making and negotiation of migration-related boundaries will, therefore, entail various discursive techniques of temporary meaning stabilisation (Amelina, 2020), including prototypical (and often stereotypical) imaginations of 'movers' and 'stayers', as well as widely shared narratives that mirror dominant understandings of the 'problem' that migration 'poses'. One of the goals of an intersectional regime perspective will therefore necessarily be to analyse the interplay of discursive orders with social relations and societal institutions – in Foucauldian terms, the nexuses of power and knowledge.

How do boundaries, thus understood, relate to borders? In line with recent border regime studies, we conceive of borders as institutions and technologies that selectively regulate entry, movement, and settlement and thereby mediate access to differentiated forms of membership (de Genova and Peutz, 2010; Mezzadra and Neilson, 2012; Walters, 2006). Boundaries, then, provide logics and classifications that inform the establishment of borders, which in turn stabilise the meaning of boundaries as dominant inequality-producing social classifications. Social classifications and related hierarchical boundaries are thus part and parcel of migration regimes.

---

[4] In line with the current literature, the terms classification and categorization are closely related in our usage. They mutually imply each other, but have somewhat different connotations. Classification emphasizes the logics and processes of assigning individuals to categories, while 'categorization' focuses more on the definition of single groups/classes.

490 Regimes of Intersection

They shape concrete political technologies, and they mediate the effects that policies and politics impose on individual life chances and life courses. Hence, we may speak of the performativity of boundaries in migration regimes, allowing us to view migration regimes as sets of regulatory processes that 'do migration', in that they transform movers (and often even non-movers) into 'migrants' in need of regulation (Amelina, 2020).

The interplay between boundaries and borders is a logical focal point for intersectional analyses of migration regimes. Such an explicitly intersectional regime perspective provides a theoretical foundation as well as concrete heuristics for relating what are usually treated as disparate aspects (different fields of practice, different scales of policy making, various narratives etc.) while at the same time framing these aspects as part of an overarching problematic: the governing of mobilities and mobile subjectivities in contexts of multiply overlapping social inequalities. In this short article, we aim to promote this general approach without claiming to furnish it in any finished form.

Existing studies on intersectional dynamics in migration contexts have discussed the gendered, ethnicised/racialised, and class-related effects of political regulations of borders and mobilities once they are established. (e.g. Bastia, 2014; Fathi, 2017; Stypińska and Gordo, 2018; Grosfoguel et al., 2015; Lutz, 2017; Schwenken, 2018). Our key argument is that a comprehensive intersectional analysis of migration regimes needs to address two further crucial issues. These issues are, first, the emergence of boundaries and borders and, second, the processes of enactment and implementation through which these orders structure mobilities and inequalities. The former aspect requires an investigation of often counterintuitive interplays of political rationalities in migration contexts; the latter begs the question of how different fields of practice are involved in translating political frameworks into social realities.

Intersecting rationalities: The tension ridden logics of economisation, securitisation and humanitarianisation

In this section, we illustrate the relevance of analysing the intersectional dynamics of the political rationalities that underlie the development of migration regulations, with a focus on the current European context. The notion of political rationalities follows Foucault's analysis of neoliberal governmentality (Foucault, 2009; 2010). Three dominant forms of thematising migration can be discerned in the context of liberal nation-states: (i) utilitarian logics that render migration a question of cost–benefit calculations, or the economisation narrative (Menz, 2009); (ii) security logics that posit migration as a threat to social security, national identity, and public order, or the securitisation narrative (Bigo, 2002; Huysmans, 2006); and (iii) humanitarian logics that discuss migration against the background assumption of shared humanity, or the humanitarian narrative (Fassin, 2011a). Each of these rationalities is reflected in common narratives on "what kind of problem" migration is supposed to be. Importantly, these three rationalities are institutionally anchored in the form of the liberal nation-state; they correspond to "the three pillars of governmentality, that is, economy, police, and humanitarianism" (Fassin, 2011b, 221). Each of these rationalities already carries intersectional implications. Most importantly, their interplay shows important interlocking effects.

The economisation narrative is, on the surface, typically mobilised to justify immigration, for example, by referring to demographic change or labour market shortages. In this vein, the official European Union (EU) rhetoric explicitly relates 'prosperity' and 'competitiveness' to the rhetoric of free movement (Menz and Caviedes, 2010). Typically, economisation narratives constitute boundaries that allow to hierarchically classify migrants into groups that are imagined as necessarily having different legal positions and enjoying different sets of rights, according to their 'skill levels' (Horvath, 2014b). 'Skill' functions here as a code for 'class' and is also deeply marked by neocolonial orders and discourses, already pointing to an important aspect of intersectionality. [5] The economised treatment of migration also entails gender-related classifications. For mobile EU citizens, for example, gender becomes articulated in the breadwinner approach (Anthias et al., 2013), which affects family members of mobile EU citizens. Classifications around gender become even more significant for non-EU labour migrants when it comes to the process of family reunification.

The securitisation narrative, prominent in Europe from the 1920s onwards, has become highly dominant since the end of the bipolar, post-WWII world order, especially in the context of the 'war against terrorism' that emerged at the turn of the millennium (Huysmans, 2006). Supported by security professionals such as police forces and secret services (Bigo, 2002), the securitisation of migration has been a key element of a general restructuring of security policies over recent decades. The prescribed need for 'exceptional measures' amounted to a massive expansion of deportation and detention policies (de Genova and Peutz, 2010). Again, the narrative of securitisation has important intersectional underpinnings and entails classifications regarding ethnicity/race and gender as well as references to postcolonial and class orders, all of which become attached to questions of spatial autonomy and imaginations of transnational threats. This interplay of classifications is particularly visible in media figures such as the 'aggressive male asylum seeker', often also presented as 'a welfare tourist' 'misusing asylum regulations', whose spatial autonomy needs to be limited, and whose supposed transnational networks are depicted as a potential danger (Dietze, 2016; Wetterich, 2018). Securitising and economising rationalities are already related in the resulting legal orders: the lower the prospective economic value attached to a migrant category, the greater the probability that the social, spatial, and temporal autonomy of that category will be constrained.

Although the economisation and the securitisation of migration are often presented as expressing opposing political standpoints, it is their very intersectionality that drives the development and establishment of political regulations. For example, Horvath (2014b) shows how recently established European labour migration programmes that may seem to follow a purely economising logic (emphasising the need for and benefits of migration) actually hinge on the preceding and simultaneous securitisation of migration: The latter forms the background against which specific criteria become accepted as legitimate grounds for differentiating fundamental rights. The massive securitisation of migration after 1989 was thus a necessary precondition for introducing points-based systems that use criteria such as education, language knowledge, or age as a way of grouping migrants into hierarchical orders, as well as for designing temporary worker programmes (seasonal work) that are marked by the almost all-encompassing deprivation of fundamental rights. Hierarchical boundaries introduced under securitised preconditions thus become invested and utilised in the border policies of utilitarian migration programmes. It is the

---

[5] In this context, another important example can be noted: the widespread de-skilling of so-called (highly-) skilled migrants. This is clearly a highly intersectional phenomenon: While mostly male and mostly white intercorporate 'ex-pats' may experience their transnational mobility as upward mobility, those 'skilled' migrants coming from the global South or in gendered work contexts are far more likely to end up in relatively disadvantaged positions that do not correspond to formal qualifications and previous work experience.

intersectional dynamic between different political rationalities that yields and justifies specific forms of political regulation.

What about the third political rationality, humanitarianism? Could humanitarian narratives provide a basis for circumventing the intersectional dynamics that evolve between economising and securitising political logics? From an intersectional regime perspective, the answer to this question will have to be nuanced, mirroring the complexity of humanitarian thought in Western modernity (Fassin, 2011a). By referring to images of shared humanity and universal rights, these humanitarian narratives seem to carry the potential for tempering the effects of hierarchical boundaries between 'Us' and 'Them'. However, at the intersections of humanitarianisation with other political rationalities there evolve new detrimental patterns of boundary-making within current European migration regimes. First, the discursive images of 'asylum seekers' and 'refugees' become articulated in terms of class, gender, ethnicity/race, and space classifications. 'True' forced movers are imagined to be of low social class within their sending countries, where they lack opportunities, with no choice but to move to another country. These images are also highly gendered, since the notion of 'enforcement' generates images of vulnerable and passive subjects – particularly in images of victimised 'women and children' (Gray and Franck, 2018; Johnson, 2011; McPherson, 2015; Neikirk, 2017). Second, these images of vulnerability are inversely related to degrees of (pseudo-economised) 'deservingness', meaning that mobile men can be more easily ethnicised/racialised and, consequently, subject to securitised regulations: this interplay of political logics explains the paradoxical constellation that those seeking the 'internationally protected' legal status of 'refugee' face the highest restrictions regarding spatial autonomy and other social rights (Casati, 2018; Holmes and Castaneda, 2016; Holzberg et al., 2018; Ratfisch, 2015; Sales, 2002). Third, because of the status of exceptional emergency inherent in asylum narratives, the field of allegedly humanitarian migration has over the past decades become a laboratory for developing and establishing ever more draconian measures that are then transferred to other fields of migration politics (Horvath, 2014a). Humanitarian narratives thus are deeply involved in the evolution of borders and boundaries, up to the introduction of militarized detention and deportation regimes (Fassin, 2011b).

If we shift our attention from the intersectional effects of regulations to the political rationalities that yield them, a whole new set of relevant intersectionalities arises. These are intersectionalities in the true sense of the word. Each of the discussed political rationalities has its own dynamics and is anchored in institutions and fields of practice in its own way. While each of the rationalities already implies intersectional classifications and related hierarchical boundaries, it is the interplay between different rationalities that has the most striking effects: securitisation gives rise to boundaries that are then used for economised border politics, and humanitarian narratives become battlefields in which new detention and deportation policies are developed. Borders and boundaries become related in manifold ways in and through this intersectional interplay of political rationalities: border assemblages generate boundaries that in turn become effective in technologies and dispositifs of bordering, a transversal process that spans different fields of practice.

Intersecting enactments: The example of educational participation and classification in the age of migration politics

The plurality of political rationalities on migration issues has important implications that are often missed. It points to the intersecting involvement of various (border-related) societal institutions in migration regimes, from securitising actors such as the police to economising organisations such as entrepreneurs associations to humanitarian institutions such as social work. Besides being entangled in the *formation* of regulations, these and other fields of practice also play a crucial role when it comes to *implementing* and *enacting* boundaries and borders. The concrete effects of migration regimes on individual life chances are hence mediated by institutions and practices which may seem far detached from politics in a narrow sense. Recent scholarships provides first insights on these entanglements for fields such as administration (Dahlvik, 2017) or the law (Eule, 2019). In the following, we illustrate the intersectional political entanglements involved in the everyday enactment of borders and boundaries using the example of education. We point to a number of important interplays between political and educational dynamics, most of which are so far barely researched and understood.

Education, as a field of practice, is heavily entangled with borders and boundaries. As will be discussed in the following, borders directly affect educational participation – border orders structure student populations. At the same time, schools themselves must be seen as bordering institutions. Their role in this regard is in the field of 'social citizenship' (Marshall, 1950; Moses, 2017). Their key function is to assign social status and to select and evaluate students for specific educational tracks. Schools are 'sorting machines' (Domina et al. 2017), that are deeply engaged in producing and transforming durable 'categorical inequalities' (Tilly, 1999). In fulfilling these functions, educational institutions and practices are interrelated with the dynamics of migration regimes in many ways (Horvath 2018; 2019). Most importantly, the boundaries that structure public and political discourse become effective in the everyday sorting and classification activities of schools in often unforeseen ways. Educational institutions thereby make hierarchical boundaries consequential and meaningful – it is through organisations such as schools that discursive boundaries actually structure life chances. This, however, is not a straightforward, but a highly complex, intersectional process.

Take the example of participation in education systems (Hochschild and Cropper, 2010). Schools and teachers in the current European context are confronted with an already bounded population that has been filtered and differentiated by migration regimes. For example, children of most temporary migrants will never have access to the education system of the receiving country, an issue that has so far been completely under the radar of education research in spite of the dramatic rise of temporary migrant worker programmes all over the global North and West (Henderson, 2004; Horvath, 2014b). The exclusion of these children is an extreme consequence of a profound rearrangement of social class, migrant status, and ethnicity/race in education contexts, translating a general tendency towards hierarchical stratification by European migration regimes (Engbersen et al., 2017) into transnational educational inequalities. Overall, the nexus between current migration regimes and educational participation are contradictory. On the one hand, recent long-term migration is today less clearly linked to disadvantaged positions than in previous decades; long-term settlement in the European context has become more of a middle- to upper-class phenomenon. On the other hand, already existing minority populations (often resulting from post-WWII labour migration), as well as newly arrived migrants with less secure legal statuses, find themselves in persistently and intersectionally disadvantaged positions.

Educational institutions are not merely passively faced with these developments; rather, they actively engage with and shape them. In other words, schools are not only confronted with a hierarchised body of students but may actually contribute to and reinforce hierarchical boundaries and borders. For example, mirroring trends towards positively connoted elite cosmopolitanism, hitherto monolingual school settings now increasingly encourage the use of prestigious 'cosmopolitan' foreign languages (mostly English or French) – even as an official instructional language – whereas less prestigious languages (those spoken by ethnicised/racialised minority populations) are denigrated and delegitimised in various ways. These orders of linguistic worth, again, reflect intersectional constellations of social class, ethnicity/race, belonging, and degrees of spatial autonomy in current migration regimes (Holmes et al., 2017).

The hierarchised participation of migrant children in education goes hand in hand with other practices of educational classification. For example, teachers regularly draw on extra-pedagogical boundaries for defining and handling the uncertainties that arise in everyday educational situations. In this vein, the category of 'migration background' is today routinely applied in German-speaking school contexts to make sense of students and their life worlds in an 'understanding' and individualising manner. At the same time, it is used to delimit areas of (non-)responsibility: by referring to this category, teachers feel able to 'explain' educational disadvantages and simultaneously declare them as being beyond their professional reach (Horvath, 2019).

These kinds of migration-related categories are best understood as 'entangled' (Horvath, 2018), if not outright 'intersectional': although they stem from political and public discourses, they are used in accordance with the needs and logics of educational classification. These entangled categories fulfil different 'intersectional' functions, for example allowing for communication with actors from other fields (such as social scientists or social workers). Far more importantly, they can become the anchor point for certain forms of problematising educational situations in line with political and social dynamics. Thus, the mentioned category of 'migration background' has today become fixed as a focal point of a widespread pedagogic narrative which relates the perceptions of students and their families to didactic strategies and professional self-understandings (Horvath, 2018). These forms of entangled boundary making and problematisation have important consequences because they threaten to further deteriorate the position of those who already are disadvantaged. Minority and post-migrant populations thereby face reduced chances to obtain the kind of certified educational qualification that today's migration regimes increasingly require for gaining international mobility rights.

To sum up, migration regimes are implemented and enacted by educational institutions in manifold ways. Educational institutions mediate and materialise the concrete effects of borders and boundaries on individual biographies. Border orders and boundaries become effective in schools not only through the differential selection and positioning of migrant children but also by providing discursive resources for making sense of and handling pedagogic situations. In their combination, these processes tend to exacerbate already existing intersectional inequalities. Any understanding of how education is interwoven with migration regimes needs to take the autonomous logics and structures of pedagogic practice seriously. Its partly autonomous, yet deeply politically entangled character warrants the call for an intersectional perspective. Other fields of practice can be expected to be similarly interwoven with migration regimes, but each in its own ways and corresponding to its own structures and logics.

Conclusion

This article pleads for a wide intersectional enrichment of our understanding of migration regimes. Such an approach would add to our understanding of how borders and boundaries come about, how they are interrelated, and how they develop their effects. An intersectional outlook implies to choose the manifold interplays of (relatively autonomous) actors, discourses, and institutions involved in these processes as an analytical focus. On this basis, we can understand how political rationalities that are usually treated as separate or even opposing (such as economising, securitising, and humanitarian narratives on migration) interrelate in yielding boundaries and border policies, or how the concrete effects of migration regulations on social formations evolve through an interplay of professional fields of practice, such as education.

We believe that such an intersectional regime approach offers manifold perspectives for empirical research that aims to identify and meaningfully analyse politically regulated dynamics of hierarchical boundary making, inclusion, and exclusion in our current 'age of migration' (Castles et al., 2013). Its key promise in this regard also marks the central challenge it faces: An intersectional regime perspective would provide heuristics and concepts for doing research that crosses still dominant thematic, disciplinary, and methodological boundaries within migration studies. Future research could, for example, 'follow' concrete boundaries and regulations through their stages of development from their early emergence to their more or less immediate effects, or target the subtle political and social consequences of professional practices that on first sight might seem pretty detached from the politics of borders and migration. The realisation of this potential, however, requires an openness for research that crosses and bridges established subfields of migration research that still tend to live in relative isolation from each other.

Against this background, an important promise of intersectional regime perspectives concerns their capacity to engage social actors in a dialogue concerning the political foundations and implications of their agency. This demand for reflexivity also applies to migration research itself. After all, migration scholars themselves are heavily involved in the intersectional development, negotiation, implementation, and problematisation of migration-related boundaries and borders.

References

Amelina, A. (2017). Transnationalizing Inequalities in Europe: Sociocultural Boundaries, Assemblages, Regimes of Intersection. London: Routledge.

Amelina, A. (2020). "After the reflexive turn in migration studies: Towards the doing migration approach." Population, Space and Place. https://doi.org/10.1002/psp. 2368.

Anthias, F. (2001). "The material and the symbolic in theorising social stratification: Issues of gender, ethnicity and class", British Journal of Sociology 52 (3): 367–390.

Anthias, F., Kontos, M. and Morokvasic, M. (2013). Paradoxes of Integration: Female Migrants in Europe. Dordrecht: Springer Science + Business.

Badenhoop, E. (2017). "Calling for the Super Citizen: Citizenship ceremonies in the UK and Germany as techniques of subject-formation", Migration Studies, 5 (3): 409–427.

Bartels, I. (2017). "'We must do it gently': The contested implementation of the IOM's migration management in Morocco", Migration Studies, 5 (3): 315–336.

Bastia, T. (2014). "Intersectionality, migration and development", Progress in Development Studies, 14 (3): 237–248.

Becker-Schmidt, R. (2007). " 'Class', 'gender', 'ethnicity', 'race': Logiken der Differenzsetzung, Verschränkungen von Ungleichheitslagen und gesellschaftliche Strukturierung". In C. Klinger, G. A. Knapp and B. Sauer (eds) Achsen der Ungleichheit: Zum Verhältnis von Klasse, Geschlecht und Ethnizität, Frankfurt am Main: Campus.

Bell Hooks [i. e. Gloria Jean Watkins] (1981). Ain't I a Woman: Black Women and Feminism. Boston, MA: South End Press.

Bigo, D. (2002). "Security and immigration: Toward a critique of the governmentality of unease", Alternatives: Global, Local, Political, 27: S63–S92.

Boyer, R. and Saillard, Y. (eds.) (2002). Régulation Theory: The State of the Art. London: Routledge.

Brug, W. van der, D'Amato, Ruedin, D. and Berkhout, J. (eds.) (2015). The Politicisation of Migration. London: Routledge.

Casati, N. (2018). "How cities shape refugee centres: 'Deservingness' and 'good aid' in a Sicilian town", Journal of Ethnic and Migration Studies, 44 (5): 792–808.

Castles, S., de Haas, H. and Miller, M.J. (2013). The Age of Migration: International Population Movements in the Modern World (5th ed.). Houndmills: Palgrave Macmillan.

Collins, P.H. (2000). Black Feminist Thought: Knowledge, Consciousness, and the Politics of Empowerment (2nd ed.). New York: Routledge.

Dahlvik, J. (2018). Inside Asylum Bureaucracy: Organizing Refugee Status Determination in Austria. Cham: Springer Open.

de Genova, N. and Peutz, N. (eds.) (2010). The Deportation Regime: Sovereignty, Space, and the Freedom of Movement. Durham, NC: Duke University Press.

Dietze, G. (2016). "Ethnosexismus: Sex-Mob-Narrative um die Kölner Sylvesternacht", movements, 2 (1): 177–185.

Domina, T./ Penner, A and Penner, E. (2017). Categorical Inequality: Schools As Sorting Machines. Annual Review of Sociology, 43, 311-330.

El-Kayed, N. and Hamann, U. (2018). "Refugees' access to housing and residency in German cities: Internal border regimes and their local variations", Social Inclusion, 6 (1): 135–146.

Engbersen, G., Leerkes, A., Scholten, P. and Snel, E. (2017). "The intra-EU mobility regime: Differentiation, stratification and contradictions", Migration Studies, 5 (3): 337–355.

Esping-Andersen, G. (1990). The Three Worlds of Welfare Capitalism. Princeton, NJ: Princeton University Press.

Eule, T., Borrelli, L.M., Lindberg, A. and Wyss, A. (2018). Migrants Before the Law. Contested Migration Control in Europe. Berlin: Springer.

Fassin, D. (2011a). Humanitarian Reason. A Moral History of the Present. Los Angeles: University of California Press.

Fassin, D. (2011b). Policing Borders, Producing Boundaries. The Governmentality of Immigration in Dark Times, Annual Review of Anthropology, 40: 213-226.

Fathi, M. (2017). Intersectionality, Class and Migration: Narratives of Iranian Women Migrants in the U.K. New York: Palgrave Macmillan.

Foucault, M. (2009). Security, Territory, Population: Lectures at the Collège de France, 1977–78. Houndmills: Palgrave Macmillan.

Foucault, M. (2010). The Birth of Biopolitics: Lectures at the Collège de France, 1978–79. New York: Palgrave Macmillan.

Gray, H.R.C. and Franck, A.K. (2018). "Refugees as/at risk: The gendered and racialised underpinnings of securitisation in British media narratives", Security Dialogue (in press).Green, A. (1990). The Social Origins of National Education Systems. Palgrave Macmillan.

Grosfoguel, R., Oso, L. and Christou, A. (2015). " 'Racism', intersectionality and migration studies: Framing some theoretical reflections. Identities, 22 (6): 635–652.

Hammar, T. (2007). "The Politicisation of Immigration". In T. Abbas and F. Reeves (eds.) Immigration and Race Relations: Sociological Theory and John Rex. London: I.B. Tauris.

Henderson, R. (2004). Educational issues for children of itinerant seasonal farm workers: a case study in an Australian context. International Journal of Inclusive Education, 8(3), 293–310. https://doi.org/10.1080/1360311042000257708

Hochschild, J.L. and Cropper, P. (2010). "Immigration regimes and schooling regimes: Which countries promote successful immigrant incorporation?" The School Field, 8 (1): 21–61.

Holmes, P., Fay, R. and Andrews, J. (2017). "Education and migration: Languages foregrounded", Language and Intercultural Communication, 17 (4): 369–377.

Holmes, S.M. and Castaneda, H. (2016). "Representing the 'European refugee crisis' in Germany and beyond: Deservingness and difference, life and death", American Ethnologist, 43 (1): 12–24.

Holzberg, B., Kolbe, K. and Zaborowski, R. (2018). "Figures of crisis: The delineation of (un)deserving refugees in the German media", Sociology, 52 (3): 534–550.

Horvath, K. (2014a). Policing the Borders of the 'Centaur State': Deportation, Detention, and Neoliberal Transformation Processes – The Case of Austria. Social Inclusion, 2(3), 113-123.

Horvath, K. (2014b). Securitisation, economisation and the political constitution of temporary migration: The making of the Austrian seasonal workers scheme. Migration Letters, 11(2), 154-170.

Horvath, K. (2018). Fixed Narratives and Entangled Categorisations: Educational Problematizations in Times of Politicised and Stratified Migration. Social Inclusion, 6(3), 237-247.

Horvath, K. (2019). Migration Background – Statistical Classification and the Problem of Implicitly Ethnicising Categorisation in Educational Contexts. Ethnicities, 19(3), 558-574.

Horvath, K., Amelina, A., and Peters, K. (2017). Re-thinking the politics of migration. On the uses and challenges of regime perspectives for migration research. Migration Studies, 5(3), 301-314.

Huysmans, J. (2006). The Politics of Insecurity: Fear, Migration and Asylum in the EU. Abingdon: Routledge.

Johnson, H.L. (2011). "Click to donate: Visual images, constructing victims and imagining the female refugee", Third World Quarterly, 32 (6): 1015–1037.

King, D.K. (1988). "Multiple jeopardy, multiple consciousnesses: The context of a black feminist ideology", Signs, 14 (1): 42–72.

Krasner, S.D. (1982). "Structural causes and regime consequences: Regimes as intervening variables", International Organization, 36 (2): 185–205.

Lamont, M. and Molnár, V. (2002). "The study of boundaries in the social sciences", Annual Review of Sociology, 28: 167–195.

Lutz, H. (2017). "Care as a fictitious commodity: Reflections on the intersections of migration, gender and care regimes", Migration Studies, 5 (3): 356–368.

Lutz, H., Herrera Vivar, M.T. and Supik, L. (2011). "Framing Intersectionality: An Introduction". In H. Lutz, M.T. Herrera Vivar and L. Supik (eds.) Framing Intersectionality: Debates on a Multi-Faceted Concept in Gender Studies. Farnham: Ashgate.

Marshall, T.H. (1950). Citizenship and Social Class. London: Pluto Press.

McPherson, M. (2015). Refugee Women, Representation and Education: Creating a Discourse of Self-Authorship and Potential. Abingdon: Routledge.

Menz, G. (2009). The Political Economy of Managed Migration: Nonstate Actors, Europeanization, and the Politics of Designing Migration Policies. Oxford: Oxford University Press.

Menz, G. and Caviedes, A. (eds.) (2010). Labour Migration in Europe. Houndmills: Palgrave Macmillan.

Mezzadra, S. and Neilson, B. (2012). "Between inclusion and exclusion: On the topology of global space and borders", Theory, Culture & Society, 29 (4/5): 58–75.

Moses, J. (2017). "Social citizenship and social rights in an age of extremes: T. H. Marshall's social philosophy in the longue durée", Modern Intellectual History. doi:10.1017/S1479244317000178

Neikirk, A.M. (2017). "Expectations of vulnerability in Australia", Forced Migration Review, (54): 63–65.

Pott, A./, Rass, C. and Wolff, F. (eds.) (2018). Was ist ein Migrationsregime? What Is a Migration Regime? Wiesbaden: Springer VS.

Ratfisch, P. (2015). "Zwischen nützlichen und bedrohlichen Subjekten: Figuren der Migration im europäischen 'Migrationsmanagement' am Beispiel des Stockholmer Programms", movements, 1 (1).

Sainsbury, D. (2006). "Immigrants' social rights in comparative perspective: Welfare regimes, forms in immigration and immigration policy regimes", Journal of European Social Policy, 16 (3): 229–244.

Sales, R. (2002). "The deserving and the undeserving? Refugees, asylum seekers and welfare in Britain", Critical Social Policy, 22 (3): 456–478.

Schwenken, H. (2018). "Intersectional migration regime analysis: Explaining gender-selective labor emigration regulations". In A. Pott, C. Rass and F. Wolff (eds.) Was ist ein Migrationsregime? What Is a Migration Regime?. Wiesbaden: Springer VS.

Sciortino, G. (2004). "Between phantoms and necessary evils: Some critical points in the study of irregular migrations to Western Europe". In A. Böcker, B. de Hart and I. Michalowski (eds.) Migration and the Regulation of Social Integration. Osnabrück: Institute for Migration Research and Intercultural Studies.

Stypińska, J. and Gordo, L.R. (2018). "Gender, age and migration: An intersectional approach to inequalities in the labour market", European Journal of Ageing, 15 (1): 23–33.

Tilly, C. (1999). Durable Inequality. Berkeley: University of California Press.

Walby, S. (2009). Globalisation and Inequalities: Complexity and Contested Modernities. London: Sage.

Walters, W. (2006). "Border/control", European Journal of Social Theory, 9 (2): 187–203.

Wetterich, C. (2018). Gendered Security Perspectives of the Refugee 'Crisis' in the British and German Media: A Securitisation of Gender? ABI Working Paper No. 9. Freiburg: Arnold Bergstraesser Institute.

Wimmer, A. (2013). Ethnic Boundary Making: Institutions, Power, Networks. Oxford: Oxford University Press.

July 2020
Volume: 17, **No**: 4, pp. 499 – 509
ISSN: 1741-8984
e-ISSN: 1741-8992
www.migrationletters.com

MIGRATION
LETTERS

First Submitted: 11 February 2019 Accepted: 25 January 2020
DOI: https://doi.org/10.33182/ml.v17i4.700

Cross-border Migration and Gender Boundaries in Central Eastern Europe – Female Perspectives

Ágnes Erőss[1], Monika Mária Váradi[2], and Doris Wastl-Walter[3]

Abstract

In post-Socialist countries, cross-border labour migration has become a common individual and family livelihood strategy. The paper is based on the analysis of semi-structured interviews conducted with two ethnic Hungarian women whose lives have been significantly reshaped by cross-border migration. Focusing on the interplay of gender and cross-border migration, our aim is to reveal how gender roles and boundaries are reinforced and repositioned by labour migration in the post-socialist context where both the socialist dual-earner model and conventional ideas of family and gender roles simultaneously prevail. We found that cross-border migration challenged these women to pursue diverse strategies to balance their roles of breadwinner, wife, and mother responsible for reproductive work. Nevertheless, the boundaries between female and male work or status were neither discursively nor in practice transgressed. Thus, the effect of cross-border migration on altering gender boundaries in post-socialist peripheries is limited.

Keywords: *cross-border migration; gender roles; gender boundaries; Central Eastern Europe; dual-earner model.*

Introduction

In the countries of the former Socialist bloc, where international mobility was strictly controlled by the state for decades,[4] cross-border migration has more recently emerged as a significant social phenomenon, a common individual and family livelihood strategy affecting almost all social strata as well as men and women. Migration continues to be highly dependent on border regimes regulating cross-border movements of people.[5] While state borders between EU states have lost their importance as barriers as a result of EU accession and especially the establishment of the Schengen border-regime system, their permeability has dramatically decreased towards non-EU states like Serbia and Ukraine (Armbruster and Meinhof, 2011; Baggio 2015), especially following the refugee movement in 2015 (Paasi et al., 2018). These border regimes result in the 'hierarchisation of mobility rights' (Zbinden et al., 2016:8.) among Central Eastern European (CEE)

---

[1] Ágnes Erőss, Geographical Institute Research Centre for Astronomy and Earth Sciences, Budapest, Hungary. E-mail: eross.agnes@csfk.mta.hu.

[2] Monika Mária Váradi, Institute for Regional Studies, Budapest, Hungary. E-mail: varadim@mta-rkk-tko.hu.

[3] Doris Wastl-Walter, Professor Emerita, University of Bern, Switzerland. E-mail: wastl@giub.unibe.ch.

[4] When referring to strict control, we mean legislative measures as well as the geographical scope of mobility. For instance in Hungary, two different passports were introduced during the Socialism, one valid only for traveling inside the Eastern Bloc while visiting family in the western border zone bordering Austria required special documents because it was under military control. In Transcarpathia as it was the western border region of the Soviet Union, the border was thus heavily militarized and more or less sealed, which meant that cross-border migration was minimal.

[5] The term 'border (migration or mobility) regimes' refers to practices of regulation by which nation states control (restrict or facilitate) cross-border mobility of people, but also to normative and discursive orders inherent in these regimes. Border regimes (re-) produce global hierarchies of power and inequalities (see Horvath et al., 2017; Faist, 2014).

countries. For example, citizens of Hungary have the right of free movement within the EU, are allowed to cross national borders without being controlled, and may seek employment in other EU member states whereas those who live in the westernmost region of Ukraine called Transcarpathia face restrictions and often time-consuming controls when crossing the border to any of their directly neighbouring countries. Since 2011, when Hungary introduced preferential re-naturalisation, thousands of Transcarpathians obtained Hungarian citizenship (and its passport), which guarantees them equality in accessing the EU labour market (Tátrai et al., 2017; Erőss et al., 2018).

In the present article, we introduce two ethnic Hungarian women, Ilona and Hanna, whose lives have been significantly reshaped by cross-border labour migration in diverse ways. Our aim in analysing the semi-structured interviews conducted with the two women[6] about the same age (approximately 60) is to reveal how gender roles and boundaries are reinforced and repositioned by cross-border labour migration in the post-socialist context where both the socialist dual-earner model and conventional ideas of family and gender roles simultaneously largely prevail (Palenga-Möllenbeck and Lutz 2016; Gal and Klingman 2000).

From the large pool of interviews, we chose these two specific women because they presented very strong agency in their narratives. We identify agency as a crucial factor that empowered them to actively negotiate, reposition and shift gender boundaries within their families during certain periods of their life courses.[7] Their life and labour stories share many similarities. Both live in peripheral settlements: Ilona in Knightfield,[8] a village situated in Transcarpathia, Ukraine, where autochthonous ethnic Hungarians co-exist with Ukrainians. Hanna lives in Poppyfield, a settlement in the southern border region of Hungary. Both were born and started to work during the socialist regime when inhabitants typically used to work locally or in nearby settlements. In both villages, seeking labour in foreign countries has become a locally accepted and widely practised living strategy as a result of geopolitical and economic processes, such as the collapse of the socialist economy in both countries, the economic crisis after 2008, or more recently, following the Euromaidan in Ukraine. However, the local inhabitant's cross-border migration trajectories have developed differently: In Knightfield (Transcarpathia, Ukraine), where Ilona lives, the general pattern is that males migrate to foreign countries, just as Ilona's husband does. In contrast, in Poppyfield, Hungary, mostly women, once including Hanna, are engaged in cross-border labour migration. Migration is thus an essential factor in their lives: it has forced them to rearrange their lives in order to be able to migrate on their own (Hanna) or support their family members to migrate (Ilona).

---

[6] In Hungary, the research project 'International Migration from Hungary and its Impacts on Rural Society' (2015-2018) was founded by NKFIH/OTKA (K111 969). Within this project, one research site was a village at the Hungarian-Serbian border where 19 interviews were conducted with women who worked as live-in migrant care workers in Austria and Germany either at the time of the research or prior to it. The research in Transcarpathia, Ukraine was carried out in the frame of 'Studying the assimilation of the Transcarpathian Hungarian Diaspora Community' supported by Bethlen Gábor Alapkezelő. The aim of the project was to map everyday socio-economic circumstances of autochthonous ethnic Hungarian diaspora communities in Transcarpathia, focusing on the processes of assimilation of the Hungarian communities. In five settlements, 85 semi-structured and expert interviews were conducted. Because the aim and scope of the two research projects were completely different, the present article only offers the analysis of the labour stories of the two selected women and the study will not reflect on more general changes and processes on gender roles in the local community that were taking shape as a consequence of cross-border migration.

[7] Unfortunately, we did not have the possibility of interviewing their husbands; thus we cannot interpret the interplay of cross-border migration and gender boundaries from a male perspective.

[8] In this article, the names of the settlements and women have been anonymised and their exact age is not specified to protect their privacy.

In our article, we argue that both male and female cross-border migration has accelerated various shifts in these families' lives. Cross-border migration challenged these women to pursue diverse strategies to balance their roles of breadwinner, wife, and mother responsible for reproductive work. To a certain extent, they managed to reposition[9] gender roles and boundaries in their families. However, these strategies are constrained by economic and social characteristics of peripheral CEE regions (i.e. limited and unequal access to a 'proper' job for women) as well as by prevailing, conventional gendered values, norms, expectations and practices which have not been questioned by these women themselves. Thus, our analysis, focusing on the *interplay of gender and cross-border migration*, points to the ambivalence of gender boundaries in the post-socialist context.

Theoretical framework: cross-border migration and gender boundaries

Migration studies have paid special attention to the question of how migration in general, and migration of women in particular, affects traditional roles and responsibilities in families as well as gender relations in the sending communities (see Lutz, 2011; Fedyuk, 2015; Parreñas, 2001, 2005, 2013). While the migration of men has only a limited structural impact on gender roles, and may even reproduce them, the migration of women has larger potential to alter them, but rather in the form of long term, inter-generational, and gradual change (see de Haas, 2009: 40-41 for an overview). The international literature on 'left-behind' women primarily analyses how male out-migration impacts women's agency and power position in their marriage, family and community (Toyota et al., 2007). It has been found that male out-migration usually 'creates space for women to renegotiate gender relationships, increases decision-making power and access to and control over resources' (Saha et al., 2018:40). Some examples show that the increased authority in decision making about their private lives or family-related finances might empower women to renegotiate their position in family and local society (Jacka, 2014). Nevertheless, when women take over traditional male work and decisions, they often face disapproval from the extended family and community, and many feel powerless or are unwilling to stretch conventional gender boundaries (Wu and Ye, 2016; de Haas and van Rooij, 2010). The importance of individual agency is crucial in this context: When women take over more responsibilities and decisions previously under the auspices of male family members, they may often not perceive this state as 'emancipation,' i.e. as making independent and conscious choices against prevailing norms on gender roles (de Haas and van Rooij, 2010: 60). Thus, their narratives may lack, or only indirectly refer to, shifts in gender power positions as a result of a conscious strategy; it is researchers who perceive and account for these shifts when they analyse the narratives.

Both male and female migration can actually engender crossing, transgressing, negotiating, and shifting gender boundaries, defined as 'complex structures – physical, social, ideological, and psychological – which establish the differences and commonalities between women and men, among women, and among men, shaping and contrasting the behaviour of each gender group' (Gerson and Peiss, 1985:318). Furthermore, gender boundaries are comprehended both as symbolic and social constructions. Symbolic boundaries refer to the fact that in their everyday lives, people perceive and categorise behaviours, actions, activities (such as different types of work) as male or female, while social boundaries are 'objectified forms of social differences manifested in unequal access to and unequal distribution of resources (material and non-material) and social opportunities'

---

[9] Andreas Wimmer identified repositioning as one of the possible strategies of ethnic boundary making in which 'an actor seeks to change her own position within an existing hierarchical system' (Wimmer, 2008:988).

(Lamont and Molnár, 2002: 168). The distinction between breadwinning and domestic labour (that is, male 'job' and female 'work') is a salient gender boundary (Potuchek, 1997), implying inequalities in access to 'proper' work, salaries, recognition, and prestige. However, gender boundaries are not static social and symbolic constructions; rather, they are the 'result of a potentially reversible social process' (Wimmer 2009: 254), which vary across time and in different social contexts, and are subject to individual negotiations (Wimmer, 2008), (re-)created through 'dynamic, reciprocal and interdependent interactions between and among women and men' (Gerson and Peiss, 1985:318).

Contexts: patterns and trajectories of cross-border migration

Ukrainians today constitute one of the largest immigrant groups in Europe due to the intensive out-migration following the collapse of the USSR (Fedyuk and Kindler, 2016; IOM, 2013). The westernmost periphery of Ukraine, Transcarpathia has traditionally been characterised by a high level of migration and features characteristics rather specific to the region.[10] Migration in the region has been further boosted by the economic and political turmoil since 2014 and has been reinforced by the various policies to simplify the migration and legal employment of Ukrainian citizens by the nearby Visegrad 4 countries (Poland, Czechia, Slovakia, Hungary) (Drbhovlav and Seidlova, 2016; Tátrai et al., 2017; Jaroszewicz, 2018).

In contrast to Ukraine, Hungarian society was considered relatively 'immobile' in the two decades following the political-economic change in 1989. When the 2008 global crisis reached the country, the deteriorating economic situation and the insecurity of livelihood perspectives forced many Hungarians, EU citizens since 2004, to seek jobs and prosperity in Western European countries, mainly the UK, Germany and Austria (Hárs, 2016 a, b).

Here it is essential to note that in both Ukraine and Hungary, cross-border labour migration is highly gendered, because men and women enter different segments of the gender-segregated labour market in the target countries. Whereas most women find work in the care sector, men usually work as skilled and unskilled labourers in typically male sectors such as construction or meat processing (for the Southeast European context, see Zbinden et al., 2016: 12).

Different female perspectives on cross-border migration

Short biographies

Ilona

Ilona[11] was born and lives in Knightfield, a village in Transcarpathia with nearly 550 inhabitants where labour migration is dominated by men who engage in one-to-three month shifts and return home to spend one-to-two week breaks with their family. As Ilona recounts: 'We can say that only women are at home. Men all work…and they work abroad. Because there is no possibility here.'

---

[10] This includes ethnicity as a factor. For example, ethnic Hungarians and Romanians often earn their living respectively in Hungary and in Romania (see: Józwiak, 2014), whereas Ukrainians and Russians have typically sought employment elsewhere in Ukraine and Russia. In recent years, Czechia has become a favoured destination independent of ethnicity. Based on our interviews, it is important to emphasize that in peripheral, remote areas (e.g. villages in the mountains), it is primarily men who migrate for work. In some cases, this has resulted in the overrepresentation of women in the resident population, which was obvious during our field work.

[11] Ilona was almost 60 years old when the interview was conducted in 2018.

Ilona earned a degree as a librarian and used to work in the nearby town's library, so she was a member of the local elite. She married a local Hungarian man. In 1990, when she wanted to return from maternity leave, the library refused to re-employ her. Because her husband had also lost his job, the family was living in desperate conditions.[12] In 1996 to stabilise the family's situation, she and her husband saw no alternative than to go to Hungary to work as seasonal agricultural labourers and to leave behind their two sons with their grandparents. After a few months, Ilona returned,[13] but her husband remained in Hungary and has been working there ever since in construction. Their sons joined him and have been working in Hungary since 2005, while their families remained in Knightfield.

Since 1990, Ilona has been legally unemployed, but this does not mean that she is not working. Every day except Sunday, she travels to nearby settlements where she works as a housekeeper in wealthy families' homes. She also cultivates her garden and helps her daughters-in-law with their grandchildren. Additionally, she has been an elected representative of her neighbourhood in the municipal council for ten years in a row. She talks about this position with pride and perceives it as a 'proper job'[14] in that it partially rehabilitates her status as a white-collar working woman and entrusted member of the local community since she has been officially unemployed for decades.

Hanna

Hanna[15] lives in Poppyfield, a village with 1,950 inhabitants located at the Hungarian-Serbian border, where the dominant migration pattern has been the circular migration of female care workers. As one of them stated, 'Here we [the women] provide for the families, we who go abroad.'

Hanna had two children[16] when she got married to her second husband with whom they have one son. Hanna worked in a local bakery and could hardly reconcile her work with her household and child-care duties.

'I was always nervous and shouted at the children. Then at one point, my husband said, » It does not work anymore. You should stay at home! (…) The children should not grow up on the street! It is the woman's duty to stay at home! «'

Since then, about twenty years before the interview, Hanna has been officially unemployed.[17] For some time, Hanna accepted her husband's arguments that the children needed their mother's care all day, but after a while she felt apathetic: 'I wanted to work. I desired to meet other people.' Although her husband firmly opposed her aspirations, Hanna reported for seasonal agricultural work in Germany without asking her husband's agreement. During that season, Hanna fell seriously ill because of the hard working conditions. After recovering, she started working as a care worker in a German village in four-week rotation shifts. Like most local women working in Germany, she was never legally employed; moreover, neither she nor her employers showed interest in legalising her position. Between two shifts abroad she cleaned the houses of local elderly in Poppyfield and

---

[12] 'There were days when I had to figure out what I could possibly feed the kids …Some days even if I had not eaten anything, but I found a way to feed them, at least.'

[13] As she recalled during the interview, she had wanted the whole family to resettle in Hungary in the 1990s to provide a better and more secure life for their sons, but her husband resisted.

[14] At one point in the interview, she even voiced her hope that this position would be added to her actively employed years and might be counted in her pension.

[15] Hanna was nearly 60 when the interview was conducted in 2017.

[16] In contrast to Ilona, Hanna did not continue her education after finishing primary school and always performed unskilled work in the labour market.

[17] She was registered as unemployed at the labour office, which provided her a minimal level of social insurance.

at the weekends, she cooked in the elderly care home in a nearby village, without being officially employed.

When we met Hanna, she had been living in the village for three years because of the serious illness of her husband and worked in a small local food plant, legally employed but for very low wages. She planned to return to care work in Germany once her husband recovered.

Attempts at repositioning gender boundaries

Analysing the two women`s life and labour stories, we highlight the importance of both women having grown up during the socialist era, when the dual-earner family – and the formal, officially supported 'equality' of men and women on the labour market – (see Gal and Kligman, 2000; Kovács and Váradi, 2000) constituted the universal model. However, we should recall that the dual-earner model of socialism has not been able to alter conventional gender roles; the image and actual life of working women have possibly had some emancipatory effects both at the societal and family levels, but in practice, it has resulted in women's two-shift workload. They worked in their workplace and at home in the household and looked after the children while the men as the main breadwinners of the family were generally reluctant to participate in tasks and responsibilities related to domestic work (see Palenga-Möllenbeck and Lutz, 2016).

As some authors have highlighted, the traditional ideal of men as breadwinners and single providers for the family has re-appeared with the post-socialist transformation, yet in reality, families are generally in need of both parents` salaries. The tension resulting from the difference between the imagined family model and everyday reality thus questions gender roles in general (see Palenga-Möllenbeck and Lutz, 2016; Gal and Kligman 2000; Kovács and Váradi, 2000).

For Ilona as well as for Hanna, it has been self-evident to work in the legal labour market (i.e. to be employed), interrupted only by the birth of their children, but neither Ilona nor Hanna could find legal wage labour when they decided to return to the labour market. One of the structural similarities revealed by the working biographies of both women is that under the conditions of global capitalism, women in these (semi-) peripheral regions have very limited access to 'proper' work, that is, to jobs with formalised, legalised employment with a valid contract and regular payment (Ferguson and Li, 2018). Both Ilona and Hanna found jobs only in the informal sector as a housekeeper, cook and care worker for the elderly in their home countries and abroad, i.e. as domestic workers, traditionally considered 'female jobs.'[18] More generally, these structural constraints also define the limits of negotiating the boundary between male and female work. The fact that women are confined to perform only undervalued traditional female work whether unpaid at home or underpaid on the (informal) labour market confirms and reinforces the gender boundary between male (breadwinning) and female (domestic) work. In the case of Ilona, this is further underscored by the objective disparity between the economic conditions in Hungary (where her husband works) and Ukraine, especially the peripheral Transcarpathia, where wages are substantially below the Hungarian average.[19] In this context, Ilona's work is both symbolically and materially of low value because it derives from undervalued 'female work' which she performs in

---

[18] Their position in the paid but informal labour market is vulnerable, which they narratively and symbolically mitigate by emphasizing the 'familiar relationship' (Hanna) to the elderly she cared for or the 'goodness' (Ilona) of their wealthy employer families. As Ilona illustrated, 'I do work in good places, among good people. Because even among rich, there are good people.'

[19] According to official statistics, as of 1 January 2018 in Transcarpathia, the average wage was 6,799 Hryvnia (approximately 228 EUR); the same data for Hungary is 316,268 HUF (approximately 978 EUR). Source of data for Ukraine: Держстат Головне управління статистики у Закарпатській області (http://www.uz.ukrstat.gov.ua/press/2018/expr_v262.pdf/, for Hungary: https://www.ksh.hu/docs/hun/xstadat/xstadat_evkozi/e_qli029b.htmla

the informal sector in a peripheral, poor region. In contrast, Ilona's husband earns his salary in Hungary in the relatively well-paid construction sector, where he has had a stable position for twenty years. The imbalance between the spouses' labour positions is reflected in how she talks about her work, namely that she never mentions how much she earns or how her wages contribute to the family budget, whereas she found it important to mention that her husband financed her obtaining a driver's license.[20] Nevertheless, she talks about this disparity or her multiple workload without any anxiety or complaint, suggesting that she is comfortable with the circumstances.

On the other hand, the salary Hanna earned with the typical 'female job' in Germany was hardly enough to stabilise her family's economic position in the long term. This was because first, she was engaged in it for an overall period of five years, but with longer and shorter interruptions; and second, she only could earn a salary in the four-week shift rotation system.[21] Thus, her husband's wages earned in Hungary were also necessary to improve their circumstances.

Besides their paid jobs, both women fulfilled their role as housewife, mother and spouse as was requested and partially expected by their family and husbands. Because Ilona's husband provided a modest income level for her and their two sons, she stayed at home, taking care of their children and the household and cultivating her small garden. Later, when both of their sons married, she started to teach her Ukrainian daughters-in-law and her grandchildren Hungarian.[22] When Hanna was struggling with working hard in her workplace and at the same time looking after the family, she, like Ilona, quit her job and decided to dedicate her full attention to the family for a period of time. These tasks and responsibilities as mother and housewife more or less fit the traditional conception of female work in the context of post-socialist societies (see Palenga-Möllenbeck and Lutz, 2016).

None of them felt comfortable with their position as mother and housewife, confined to only performing traditional reproductive female roles. Ilona started to work as a housekeeper in multiple households. However, her words about this work may suggest that she feels embarrassed about never having managed to regain her position in the official labour market, in a 'real' work place:

'I work, but … how to put it… (…) I don't have a workplace…I do have a place to work, that is what I'm trying to say, I do have a place to work, I do work every day.'

Her explanation about work and workplaces suggests that Ilona does not consider her heavy workload and multiple workplaces as a 'proper job' (Ferguson and Li, 2018). In Ilona's interpretation, her paid work is primarily important to her mental well-being because it allows her to partially regain her status as a working woman and mitigate her social isolation (see Schaer et al., 2017:1301-1302).[23]

---

[20] 'I've received the driver's license. I mean I have it because of him, because he earned the money to cover its cost. And then we bought a car for me as well.'

[21] Generally in this system, one month's salary earned as a care worker abroad is sufficient to cover two months of the family budget at home. Hanna earned about 800-1000 EUR per shift in Germany, while other women in Poppyfield reported salaries between 1200 and 1500 EUR.

[22] She is convinced that knowing Hungarian is not only important for emotional reasons but also a necessity and asset in case of future migration. As she pressures both of their sons to resettle in Hungary with their families, she wishes to prepare and ease the life of their daughters-in-law and grandchildren by teaching Hungarian in case of a future move.

[23] She is still dreaming about launching their own family business, but her husband has never supported her idea. Thus, Ilona has done nothing to realize her dream. 'A long time ago, when we were newlyweds, I used to love to think of building a greenhouse for flowers. But my husband….he kept saying what if it didn't work out? He pulled me back.'

Hanna was able to reposition her place in her family, although she never emphasised or even mentioned that she had become the 'main breadwinner' of the family for a period of time as a consequence of her cross-border migration and earnings abroad. In fact, without her earnings abroad, the family could neither have afforded some smaller investments in the house nor have supported their grandchildren. Nonetheless, her husband did not stop arguing with her, referring to 'peace in the family' which in his opinion, was violated by Hanna's leaving the household. Hanna was constantly looking for jobs and to generate more income, while her husband insisted on the traditional male and female roles in the family.[24] Working outside of the household provided Hanna the possibility to 'break free' from the boundaries set up by her husband, reinforcing the conventional vision of gender roles. As she formulated it, care work in Germany provided her the possibility to 'step out for a while.' However, she performed her tasks as housewife and mother to satisfy her husband and youngest son in addition to working outside the household as breadwinner. She repositioned gender boundaries related to male and female work, roles and tasks, but she could manage this only at the price of work overload. Aside from financial necessity and the desire for a better quality of life, working outside the household was a means of mitigating her social isolation and of struggling for more autonomy and independence in her marriage. However, her agency was limited; while she could manage to work abroad against her husband's will for a while, and thus make decisions about how to invest her earnings at home, she was not able to persuade him to leave for Germany, which was her greatest desire. And she accepted her husband's decision. [25]

Neither Ilona nor Hanna questioned traditional gender boundaries between breadwinning and male or female domestic work. They did not use or reflect on these terms at all during the interviews. They also did not interpret as 'emancipation' their efforts to have paid work and their aspiration for less isolation and more autonomy and self-determination. Our findings are in accordance with other research; left-behind women or female migrant care workers do not describe their overburdened state or their desire for 'economic independence and a self-determined life' as 'emancipation' (Saha et al., 2018:46; Lutz, 2011:152, referring to Pessar, 2003.)

Conclusion

Based on two case studies documented in Central Eastern Europe, our aim was to analyse the interplay between cross-border migration and gender boundaries from a female perspective. The added value of our analysis lies in the comparison of two cases characterised by the alternative migration trajectories of these women (one involved in cross-border migration, the other, left-behind) whose labour and life stories nevertheless share many similarities. This allowed us to evaluate the role of cross-border migration on the efforts of repositioning and shifting gender boundaries within their families.

Ilona and Hanna, two middle-aged women, live in peripheral villages, anonymised as Knightfield (Transcarpathia, Ukraine) and Poppyfield (Hungary), where both the socialist dual-earner model and traditional ideas of family and gender roles prevail. In these settlements, the trajectories of cross-border migration are highly gendered: Whereas in Knightfield, men, like Ilona's husband, migrate to work mainly in Hungary or Czechia, in Poppyfield, women, including

---

[24] Even during the four-week shifts when Hanna worked in Germany, it was Hanna's mother who at least partly took care of him and their son by cooking and doing the laundry.

[25] She reflected on the inter-generational reproduction of gender boundaries and the limits of her own struggles by talking about her daughter. Her daughter's husband wants her to stay at home with the children, 'but she would like to go back to work. I told her it was not good so she should go back to work. I hope my daughter will get through. She is tough enough. More than I was.'

Hanna, circulate as live-in care workers in Germany or Austria. Despite this difference, we were prompted to compare the two cases because of the numerous commonalities of their labour and life stories: Both women were socialised in the socialist dual- earner model, thus making it self-evident for them to seek paid work after shorter or longer periods of absence from labour market (e.g. due to childbirth).

The transformation to capitalism drastically changed their circumstances, and they found jobs only in the informal sector of the economy as housekeeper, cook, and care worker for the elderly at home or abroad, in sum as domestic workers, traditionally considered 'female work.' Their efforts to find work and earn money on the (informal) labour market resulted in re-producing the dual-earner model, but it also meant reinstating women's two-shift work overload. Apart from financial necessity (in particular in the case of Hanna), their struggles to reposition themselves within the family aimed at regaining their status as working women, at mitigating their social isolation, and at attaining more autonomy and self-determination in their marriage.

Notably, they also did not interpret their efforts to have paid work and their aspiration for less isolation and more autonomy and self-determination as 'emancipation.' Similarly, they neither questioned nor complained about traditional gender boundaries between breadwinning and male or female domestic work; moreover, they did not even use or reflect on these terms at all during the interviews. From an analytical point of view, the observation that these women are confined to perform only undervalued traditional female work whether unpaid at home or underpaid in the (informal) labour market confirms and reinforces the gender boundary between male (breadwinning) and female (domestic) work. Additionally, the way both women perceived and talked about their struggles within their families for more autonomy highlights how persistent gender boundaries can be in small, peripheral settlements in the post-socialist context. Our account demonstrates that although both women could 'break out' of being exclusively wives and mothers, the boundaries between female and male work or status were neither discursively nor in practice transgressed, explicitly negotiated, or even questioned by them.

In sum, we argue that the most important factors determining these women's positions are (1) the structural constraints characteristic of the post-socialist context in peripheries, (2) the ambivalence deriving from the symbolic and practical persistence of both the socialist dual-earner and traditional models of male and female roles and tasks within families, and (3) their individual agency. Furthermore, the effects of cross-border migration, whether male or female, on altering gender boundaries are limited; the struggles for repositioning boundaries might be partly successful but only at the price of reproducing work overload, which remains accepted and unquestioned by both men and women.

References

Armbruster, H. and Meinhof, U. H. (2011). "Introducing Borders, Networks, Neighbourhoods: Conceptual Frames and Social Practices", In: Armbruster, H. and Meinhof, U. H. (eds.) Negotiating Multicultural Europe. Borders, Networks, Neighbourhoods, Palgrave MacMillan, 1-24.

Baggio, F. (2015). "Reflections on EU border policies: human mobility and borders – ethical perspectives", In: van der Velde, M. and van Naerssen, T. Mobility and Migration Choices, London, Routledge, 167-182.

De Haas, H. (2009). Mobility and Human Development. Human Development Research Paper 2009/1, United Nations Development Programme Human Development Report, Available: http://hdr.undp.org/sites/default/ files/ hdrp_2009_01_rev.pdf

De Haas, H. and van Rooij A. (2010). "Migration as Emancipation? The Impact of Internal and International Migration on the Position of Women Left Behind in Rural Morocco", Oxford Development Studies, 38 (1): 43-62. https://doi.org/10.1080/136008110903551603

Drbhovlav, D. and Seidlova, M. (2016). "Current Ukrainian migration to Czechia: Refuge for economic migrants rather than for refugees", In: D. Drbohlav and M. Jaroszewicz (eds.), Ukrainian migration in times of crisis: Forced and labour mobility, Prague: Charles University, Faculty of Science, Department of Social Geography and Regional Development, 95-127.

Erőss Á., Kovály K., Tátrai P. (2018). "The impact of Ukraine's crisis on migratory flows and Hungary's kin-state politics", In: Wintzer J, Filep B (eds.), Geographie als Grenzüberschreitung: Festschrift für Prof. Dr. Doris Wastl-Walter, Bern: Geographische Gesellschaft Bern, 125-137.

Faist, Th. (2014). "On the transnational social question: How social inequalities are reproduced in Europe", Journal of European Social Policy, Vol. 24 (3): 207-222. DOI: 10.1177/0958928714525814, Available: https://www.en.cgs.aau.dk/digitalAssets/151/151083_tsq_europe_jesp_2014.pdf

Ferguson, J. and Li, T. M. (2018). Beyond the "Proper Job:" Political-economic Analysis after the Century of Labouring Man. Working Paper 51., Cap Town: PLAAS, UWC, Available: https://www.africaportal.org › documents › WP_51_Beyond_the_proper_job_12_Apr_2tl2_FINAL.pdf

Fedyuk, O. (2015). "Growing Up With Migration: Shifting Roles and Responsibilities of Transnational Families of Ukrainian Care Workers in Italy", In: Kontos, M. and Bonifacio, G. (eds.), Migrant Domestic Workers and Family Life: International Perspectives, Houndmills, Basingstoke, Hampshire, New York: NY Palgrave Macmillan, 109-129.

Fedyuk, O. and Kindler, M. (2016). "Migration of Ukrainians to the European Union: Background and Key Issues", In: O. Fedyuk and M. Kindler (eds.), Ukrainian Migration to the European Union. Lessons from Migration Studies, IMISCOE Research Series, Springer Open, 1-14.

Gal, S. and Kligman, G. (2000). "Introduction", In: Gal, S. and Kligman, G. (eds.), Reproducing Gender, Politics, Publics, and Everyday Life after Socialism, Princeton, New Jersey: Princeton University Press, 3-20.

Gerson, J. M. and Peiss, K. (1985). "Boundaries, Negotiation, Consciousness: Reconceptualising Gender Relations", Social Problems, 32 (4): 317-331.

Hárs, Á (2016a). "Nemzetközi vándorlás, migrációs válság", ("International mobility, migratory crisis") In: Kolosi, T. and Tóth, I. Gy. (szerk.), Társadalmi Riport 2016, TÁRKI, 351-372.

Hárs, Á. (2016b). "Elvándorlás, bevándorlás és a magyar munkaerőpiac. Jelenségek, hatások, lehetőségek", ("Migration, immigration and the Hungarian labour market. Phenomena, impacts and possibilities"), In: Kolosi, T. and Tóth, I. Gy. (szerk.): 'Társadalmi Riport 2016' TÁRKI, 243-262.

Horvath, K., Amelina, A., and Peters, K. (2017). "Re-thinking the politics of migration. On the uses and challenges of regime perspectives for migration research", Migration Studies, Volume 5, Number 3: 301-314., doi:10.1093/migration/mnx55

IOM (2013). Migration in Ukraine. Facts and figures. Available: http://www.iom.org.ua/sites/default/files/eng_ff_f.pdf. Accessed: 23.01.2019

Jacka, T. (2014). "Left-behind and Vulnerable? Conceptualising Development and Older Women's Agency in Rural China", Asian Studies Review, 38 (2): 186–204.

Jarosewicz, M. (2018). Migration from Ukraine to Poland the trend stabilises. OSW Report. Warsaw: OSW, URL: https://www.osw.waw.pl/sites/default/files/Report_Migration%20from%20Ukraine_net.pdf

Józwiak, I. (2014). "Ethnicity, Labour and Mobility in the Contemporary Borderland. A Case Study of a Transcarpathian Township", Central and Eastern European Migration Review, 3 (1): 27–39.

Kovács, K. and Váradi M. (2000). "Women's Life Trajectories and Class Formation in Hungary", In: Gal, S. and Kligman, G. (eds.), Reproducing Gender, Politics, Publics, and Everyday Life after Socialism, Princeton, New Jersey: Princeton University Press, 176-199.

Lamont, M. and Molnár, V. (2002). "The Study of Boundaries in the Social Sciences", Annual Review of Sociology, (28): 167-95. doi:10.1146/annurev.soc.28.110601.141107

Lutz, H. (2011). The New Maids: Transnational Women and the Care Economy. London - New York: Zed Books

Paasi A., Prokkola E.-K., Saarinen J., and Zimmerbauer K. (2018): Borderless worlds for whom? Ethics Moralities and Mobilities. Border Regions Series, London, Routledge

Palenga-Möllenbeck, E. and Lutz, H. (2016). "Fatherhood and Masculinities in Post-socialist Europe: The Challenges of Transnational Migration", In: M. Kilkey and E. Palenga-Möllenbeck (eds.), Family life in an Age of Migration and Mobility. Global perspectives through the life course, Palgrave MacMillen, 213-236.

Parreñas, R. S. (2001). Servants of Globalization. Women, Migration and Domestic Work. Stanford University Press.

Parreñas, R. S. (2005). Children of Global Migration. Transnational Families and Gendered Woes. Stanford University Press.

Parreñas, R. S. (2013). "The Gender Revolution in the Philippines. Migrant Mothering and Social Transformations", In: S.E. Eckstein, and A. Najam (ed.), How Immigrants Impact Their Homelands, Duke University Press, 191-212.

Pessar, P. (2003). "Engendering migration studies: the case of new immigrants in the United States", In: Hondagneu-Sotelo, P. (ed.), Gender and US Immigration. Contemporary Trends, Berkeley: University of California Press, 20-42.

Potuchek, J. (1997). Who Supports the Family: Gender and Breadwinning in Dual-Earning Marriages. Stanford, California: Stanford University Press.

Saha, S., Goswani, R. and Paul, S.J. (2018). "Recursive Male Out-migration and the Consequences at Source: A Systematic Review with Special Reference to the Left-behind Women", Space and Culture, India, 5 (3): 30-53.

Schaer, M., Dahinden, J. and Toader, A. (2017). "Transnational mobility among early-career academics: gendered aspects of negotiations and arrangements within heterosexual couples", Journal of Ethnic and Migration Studies, 43 (8): 1292-1307, DOI:10.1080/1369183X.2017.1300254

Tátrai, P., Erőss, Á., Kovály, K. (2017). "Kin-state politics stirred by a geopolitical conflict: Hungary's growing activity in post-Euromaidan Transcarpathia, Ukraine", Hungarian Geographical Bulletin, 66 (3): 203-218.

Toyota, M., Yeoh, B. S., and Nguyen, L. (2007). "Bringing the 'left behind' back into view in Asia: a framework for understanding the 'migration–left behind nexus", Population, Space and Place, 13 (3): 157-161.

Wimmer, A. (2008). The Making and Unmaking of Ethnic Boundaries: A Multilevel Approach, American Journal of Sociology, Volume 113, Number 4: 970-1022

Wimmer, A. (2009). "Herder's Heritage and the Boundary-Making Approach: Studying Ethnicity in Immigrant Societies", Sociological Theory, 27:3: 244-270.

Wu, H and Ye, J. (2016). "Hollow Lives: Women Left Behind in Rural China", Journal of Agrarian Change, 16 (1): 50–69.

Zbinden, M., Dahinden, J. and Efendic, A. (2016). "Rethinking the Debate about Diversity of Migration in South-East Europe", In: Zbinden, M., Dahinden, J. and Efendic, A. (eds.), Diversity of Migration in South-East Europe, Peter Lang, 7-34.

July 2020
Volume: 17, No: 4, pp. 511 – 520
ISSN: 1741-8984
e-ISSN: 1741-8992
www.migrationletters.com

MIGRATION
LETTERS

First Submitted: 5 February 2019 Accepted: 6 March 2020
DOI: https://doi.org/10.33182/ml.v17i4.696

The Reconfiguration of European Boundaries and Borders: Cross-border Marriages from the Perspective of Spouses in Sri Lanka

Janine Dahinden[1], Joëlle Moret[2], and Shpresa Jashari[3]

Abstract

Cross-border marriages between citizens with a migration background and spouses from non-EU countries have been politicised and restricted across Europe. This article simultaneously applies the analytical lenses of bordering and boundary work to this issue and de-centres the perspective by investigating the consequences of these restrictions not on Europe, but on a country of origin – Sri Lanka. We show that a particular symbolic boundary against cross-border marriages in European countries legitimises the externalisation of borders to the country of origin. This has important consequences for the female spouses before they even begin their journey to Europe: it challenges their life aspirations, enhances their economic dependency and precarity and directly impacts the marriage system in Sri Lanka. We argue that this situation creates a form of neo-colonial governmentality that perpetuates historically established forms of Western politics of belonging.

Keywords: Cross-border marriages; border studies; boundary work; politics of belonging.

Introduction

Archan, the director of a language institute in Colombo, Sri Lanka, describes the situation of his students, mostly women from northern Sri Lanka who come to the capital to take a language test. If they pass it, they will be permitted to join their husbands in Europe:

These women come to Colombo only for the [language] test, which they need for the visa for family reunification with their spouses living in Europe. The failure rate is very high: roughly 60 per cent need to repeat the test several times. Quite often they try to bribe me [...]. These women are under enormous pressure to pass this language test. Sometimes they threaten to commit suicide. [...] The language class costs around €120, the final exam as well. You understand that this can get very expensive? And it often happens that if a woman fails the test and everything [i.e. the visa] gets delayed, the man simply looks for another woman. This is obviously very traumatic and difficult for the women here.

This situation is a consequence of a new configuration of European borders and boundaries that is particularly visible in the regulation of cross-border marriages involving a partner in Europe and another partner from a non-EU country.

[1] Janine Dahinden, Professor in Transnational Studies, Laboratory for the Analysis of Social Processes (LAPS) and nccr – on the move, University of Neuchâtel, Switzerland. E-mail: janine.dahinden@unine.ch.
[2] Joëlle Moret, postdoctoral researcher, Laboratory for the Analysis of Social Processes (LAPS) and nccr – on the move, University of Neuchâtel, Switzerland. E-mail: Joelle.Moret@unine.ch.
[3] Shpresa Jashari, PhD-student, Laboratory for the Analysis of Social Processes (LAPS) and nccr – on the move, University of Neuchâtel, Switzerland. E-mail: shpresa.jashari@unine.ch.

A wide body of literature on marriage migration shows the entanglement of particular symbolic boundaries and the tightening of European borders. The first are constructed upon culturalised and orientalised ideas of gender (in)equality. The latter have led to a restriction of marriage migration for non-EU citizens (Block, 2014; Bonjour & De Hart, 2013; Carver, 2016; Charsley & Bolognani, 2019). By de-centring our perspective, we contribute to this literature in three ways. First, while most studies in this field are conducted in the European countries themselves and depict the consequences of this reconfiguration of European borders and boundaries for marriage migrants in Europe, we analyse the effects in a country of origin – Sri Lanka. We show that the particular symbolic boundaries created in Europe have led to reconfigured externalised and re-territorialised borders in Sri Lanka, and that these boundaries thus contribute to differentiated restrictions on Sri Lankans' ability to migrate to Europe (Mezzadra & Neilson, 2012).

Second, a wide of body of literature scrutinises the new European border regime and its exclusionary character, mainly by discussing the human costs people face on the borders of Europe or within Europe once they arrive here (De Genova, 2017; Eule, Borelli, Lindberg, & Wyss, 2018; Yuval-Davis, Wemyss, & Cassidy, 2019). We add to this literature by showing that the externalisation and reterritorialisation of borders and boundaries has important consequences for people who are still in their country of origin, even before they begin their journey to Europe.

Finally, by examining how a "good marriage" is defined in northern Sri Lanka, we show the aspirations of the Tamil women who engage in cross-border marriages. This example demonstrates the simultaneously ethnocentric and hegemonic nature of the European definition of a "legitimate" marriage, which is based on the idea of romantic love without any other interest, a definition that makes possible a form of neo-colonial governmentality that perpetuates historically established forms of Western politics of belonging.

In the following, we first introduce the research project on which this article is based. We then clarify how we conceptualise borders and boundaries in the context of marriage migration. Finally, we depict the effects of these new border and boundary practices upon Tamil spouses waiting for their visas to join their husbands in Europe. Simultaneously applying the analytical lenses of bordering and boundary work makes it possible to understand how European nation-states and the EU reproduce themselves in a globalised and unequal world by producing exclusion in people's countries of origin, before they even become migrants.

Methodology

This article is part of a larger multi-sited research project that studies cross-border marriages from the perspective of both sponsors in Switzerland and their partners in Turkey, Kosova and Sri Lanka who are in the process of applying for the visa that will allow them to join them in Europe. Turkey, Kosova and Sri Lanka were selected because these were the countries most of the spouses of our interview partners in Switzerland came from.

This article is based on data the first author collected in fieldwork conducted in Colombo and Jaffna in 2016. She conducted problem-centred and semi-directive interviews (Witzel & Reiter, 2010) with two men and 17 women who were all married to people living in a European country. The interview partners were all involved in language courses in order to obtain a visa that would allow them to join their partners in Europe. The language schools were chosen as entry points in our search for spouses married to people in Europe. The first co-author also conducted expert interviews (Meuser & Nagel, 2009) with the director of a language school, a representative from an embassy and the president of a women's NGO. The interviews were conducted in either English or Tamil with the support of an interpreter. The researcher contacted the teachers of different language schools in Colombo and Jaffna and asked them to put her in contact with students. The interviews with the students were mostly conducted during or after class and either at the school or in a café. The expert interviews were conducted at the offices of the respective representatives. The interview data was analysed according a theoretical coding procedure (Charmaz, 2001).

Bordering and boundary work: Conceptual clarifications

Theories of boundary work and contributions to border studies both examine the processes, practices and experiences of inclusion and exclusion, but through different analytical lenses. For the sake of clarity, and to thus more clearly demonstrate the ways in which they are mutually constituted, we disentangle the two concepts.

At the most general level, boundary studies aims to understand the ways otherness, membership and belonging are and have been socially produced and organised by different actors, and with what consequences (Pachucki, Pendergrass, & Lamont, 2007). The concept of boundary finds its origins in Fredrik Barth's (1969) seminal work, in which he introduced a procedural, interactional, dynamic and relational perspective to the study of ethnic group making. Later, Michèle Lamont developed a sociology of boundaries, applying Barth's ideas to other forms of group making (Lamont & Molnar, 2002). She and her colleagues understood boundaries as having both social and symbolic dimensions. In this article, when referring to boundaries we mean symbolic boundaries, which we understand as "conceptual distinctions made by social actors to categorise objects, people and practices [… that] separate people into groups and generate feelings of similarity and group membership" (Lamont & Molnar, 2002: 168). In daily interaction, actors – individuals, state agents, journalists and so on – are involved in struggles over social distinctions and categorisations that can shift symbolic boundaries.

Following the work of many scholars (Kolossov, 2005; Paasi, 2011; Wastl-Walter, 2012; Wilson & Hastings, 2012) we understand bordering processes as linked to a territory and the spatial scale of the (nation) state. Borders are not merely physical lines on a map, however. They do not represent a fixed point in space or time, but instead "symbolise a social practice or spatial differentiation" (Van Houtum & Van Naerssen, 2002, p. 126). In line with Van Houtum (2005, p. 673), we argue that borders are differentiators of socially constructed mindscapes and meanings, and that bordering processes are always entangled with ordering and othering (see also Fassin, 2011; Van Houtum & Van Naerssen, 2002). In other words, bordering is simultaneously a political project of governance and a political project of belonging (see also Yuval-Davis et al., 2019).

The construction of both European and national borders deploys symbolic boundaries to distinguish between those who do and do not belong, who to let in and with which rights (Favell, 2014; Nieswand, 2018; Wimmer, 2002). Put differently, symbolic boundaries regulate membership in terms of the distinction between "us" and "them", while borders regulate membership in legal, infrastructural and spatial terms. Both are involved in the (re)production of systems of dominance and inequality (Amelina, 2017).

Boundary making and bordering in the regulation of cross-border marriages

Throughout Western Europe, there has been a tendency to strongly politicise cross-border marriages, particularly when they involve citizens with a migrant background and a spouse from a non-EU country. Marrying a national of an EU or European Economic Area country comes with no conditions, and in this case the state perceives marriage as a contract between two individuals, although it regulates the spouses' rights and obligations vis-à-vis each other. However, in the case of a marriage between a migrant or a citizen or resident of a European country and an extra-EU spouse, marriage becomes a legal status defined and highly controlled by an intrusive state (Carver, 2016, p. 2759). Such marriages are often seen as illegitimate, problematic and in need of governmental intervention. Most Western European countries have reacted by restricting family reunification (Wray, Agoston, & Hutton, 2014), most importantly by imposing economic thresholds on sponsors and age requirements on the incoming spouses (Bonjour & Kraler, 2014; Strasser, Kraler, Bonjour, & Bilger, 2009). These restrictions mobilise symbolic boundaries and both internalise and externalise borders. Simultaneously, given Europe's highly selective migration policies, family migration has become one of the few remaining channels through which non-EU nationals can enter Europe (Moret, Andrikopoulos, & Dahinden, 2019).

Symbolic boundaries related to marriage migration

States have a hegemonic role in determining acceptable forms of marriage and family and defining how citizens should behave towards each other in the intimate context of their home (Moret et al., 2019). Family politics and marriage are a crucial element of what Nira Yuval-Davis (2006) has called the "politics of belonging". Nation-states rely on specific, gendered visions of kinship relations in order to reproduce themselves and the boundaries of the imagined nation. As Carver (2016, p. 2772) has demonstrated in her historical analysis of marriages between British citizens and aliens, although the discourse has changed over time, the substance of the argument – the need to "protect the nation's values from being over-run by cultural others" – has remained the same.

Most importantly for the argument in this article, cross-border marriages challenge European states' normative vision of the "good family". In recent decades, cross-border marriages have increasingly been perceived as "sham", "forced", "arranged" or "bogus" – illegitimate forms of union that threaten the love- and consent-based relationships supposedly characteristic of modern, Western societies (Andrikopoulos, 2019; Bonjour & De Hart, 2013).

We can identify a symbolic boundary here that results in a particular construction of otherness. First, this symbolic boundary is based upon "femonationalism" (Farris, 2017) or "gendernationalism" (Dahinden, Fischer, Menet, & Kristol, 2018): nationalist forms of politics of belonging (Hadj Abdou, 2017) become entangled with orientalised representations of the other (Dietze, 2010), and women's rights and gender equality have become the yardsticks through which to assess who is or is not eligible to belong to European (national) societies (Delphy, 2006; Korteweg & Yudakul, 2009; Phillips, 2010). Gender equality is presented as an accomplished fact in European marriages and a genuine European value.

Second, cross-border marriages are often presented as evidence of the failed integration of both the migrants or citizens with a migrant background, on the one hand, and their incoming spouses, on the other (Charsley, Bolognani, & Spencer, 2017). The framing of migrant marriages as indicative of failed integration reinforces the idea that these marriages and forms of doing family are culturally incompatible with and a threat to the host society. Being in need of integration necessarily implies that one is not a full member of the nation and hence legitimises government intervention (Block, 2014; Schinkel, 2018).

Finally, this symbolic boundary related to cross-border marriages is based on the construction of migrant women as victims, whether of their sexist culture, Islam or gender inequality. As Bonjour and De Hart (2013, p. 72) argue, representing women as vulnerable and in need of help not only legitimises state governance of intimate relationships, but also allows European politicians to demonstrate their commitment to gender equality. This complex symbolic boundary is mobilised only against non-EU migrants from specific countries. It is not mobilised against white-settler countries such as the US and Australia or other European citizens.

New forms of bordering practices regarding cross-border marriages

Importantly, this symbolic boundary is mirrored in new bordering practices in Western Europe regarding family-related migration. This symbolic boundary based on gender equality, integration and victimisation legitimises a double form of the de-territorialisation of borders (De Genova, 2017; Walters, 2006). On the one hand, most European countries have introduced measures to restrict migration through marriage. Many of these measures take place within their borders, thus constituting an internalisation of bordering (Lavanchy, 2013; Pellander, 2015; Yuval-Davis, Wemyss, & Cassidy, 2018). On the other hand, and especially important for the following, some of these measures, including pre-entry language tests, involve the externalisation of borders. Several European countries, including Germany, the United Kingdom and France, have made a language test in the country of origin a pre-condition for a family-reunification visa. The organisations responsible for these tests, such as the British Council and the Goethe Institute, become spaces where the externalised border is territorialised in the country of origin.

The official European discourses that legitimise these new bordering practices mobilise a symbolic boundary based on female victimisation and gender inequality (Block, 2019). Policymakers present these language courses as facilitating the integration and autonomy of these women, who supposedly suffer from gender inequality in their country of origin (see also Gutekunst, 2015). These language courses grant policymakers some measure of control over these intimate relationships, even before the spouses arrive in Europe.

Effects of bordering and boundary work in the Sri Lankan context

These externalised bordering practices, based on specific racialised, gendered and morally charged symbolic boundaries, have a significant impact on the future migrants. We cannot here examine the complexities of family and kinship systems and marriages in Sri Lanka. Rather, our ambition is much more modest: we first present the definition of a "good marriage" that emerged from the interviews and demonstrate how that definition contrasts with its European counterpart. Second, we demonstrate how pre-entry language tests, contrary to their postulated emancipatory intent, increase female spouses' precarity.

What is a "good marriage"? Global inequalities and the European view on marriage

Most interview partners agreed that marriage in northern Sri Lanka is often a collective decision negotiated between families in a post-war society characterised by economic deprivation. The women we interviewed described a variety of marriage types. Some were so-called love marriages, but most were arranged, by either specialised brokers or family members living in Europe.

Asha's narrative challenges the European view that only a purely love-based marriage is a good marriage (for a discussion of how European marriages are not free from "interests", see Andrikopoulos, 2019).

When asked if she was looking forward to going abroad, Asha responded as follows:

> I am pleased. I will have a husband and we will have a family, that's the part I'm looking forward to […]. But it's the first time I'll be leaving home, I'm leaving everyone, this creates insecurity for me […]. We think that if we marry someone abroad we'll be better off, economically speaking, because we have big financial problems. Also, the men here ask for a big dowry. The young men abroad, on the other hand, they don't ask for a big dowry. Sometimes they don't ask at all […]. My parents like that I'm going abroad. Because it's difficult here. The economy is not very good here. And I can help my parents.

This quote highlights the many components of the definition of a "good marriage". For many interviewees, the most important aspiration was simply to get married and have a family. Another consideration was the ability to support their family economically. The issue of a dowry was also raised often. A dowry is common in local Tamil marriages, but less so when the marriage is a cross-border one. This can be a reason for parents to try to find a husband abroad for their daughters, especially if they have more than one daughter. Many women also referred to friends who have married and migrated to Europe. Cross-border marriages have become part of the "cultural repertoire" (Swidler, 1986), demonstrating that processes of transnationalisation are deeply anchored in northern Sri Lanka.

In other words, marriage to a man abroad is seen positively: having a family and supporting one's family are intertwined drivers of the attempt to find a husband abroad. These aspirations clash with European countries' view of a legitimate marriage, which is constructed as informed only by romantic love. They also render visible the ethnocentric underpinnings of the European view and they uncover the ways in which these aspirations are embedded in long-lasting global inequalities.

The expert from the women's NGO referred to a negative aspect of such cross-border marriages that she said had only become salient in the last few years. Many families have lost control over whom they marry their daughters to. With locally arranged marriages, parents have first-hand information about a potential husband. This knowledge is often lacking when the potential husband lives thousands of kilometres away and the match is arranged with the support of a specialised broker, who, as many interviewees told us, generally checks only if the marriage partners' caste backgrounds and horoscopes are compatible. As the women's NGO expert stated:

> Women are often cheated for various reasons. Because when the proposal comes from a foreign country, the parents don't know whether there's a problem with the man. I know one case here, a daughter, she's very poor, a proposal came, and she wanted to go to the UK. Then she borrowed money, took a loan, everything, and she went. When she got there, it was a small room […] and this man had a lot of problems, and he was a drug addict. Nobody inquired about this person, and neither did the broker. He started beating her. It was terrible.

Put differently, the global inequalities that partly inform the desire for these cross-border marriages create risks for the female marriage partner.

Consequences of the externalisation of the border through pre-entry language tests

In this complex situation, the pre-entry language test directly contributes to the female marriage partner's financial dependency and precarity.

Most of the women we interviewed had grown up during the civil war, and thus during a time when the school system did not work properly. They are often poorly educated and struggle with their German or English course. As a result, they are often unable to pass the test, or only succeed after several attempts. This situation has various highly gendered consequences. First, apart from keeping them separate from their husbands for as long as several years – a human-rights concern (Strik, De Hart, & Nissen, 2013) – passing these tests requires significant economic resources. The women we talked to often live in small villages and need to relocate to Jaffna, where they mostly live with family members, to take the course. They need to pay for the language course and their trip to Colombo to take the test, as well as for the trip(s) to the embassy. It is often the husband abroad or a family member abroad who finances these expenses. Second, we were told that some husbands cancel the marriage if it takes their wife too long to obtain her visa. Some women also told us that some men only propose conditional marriages: they marry their potential wife only when she has already passed the test. Third, the teachers and directors of the schools we interviewed indicated that many women experience serious psychological problems as a result of the course, including nervous breakdowns and suicide attempts. Finally, it is becoming increasingly common for the women to be rejected by their family if the man cancels the marriage. New NGOs have been established to provide these abandoned women with care.

In other words, this externalised bordering practice, which is legitimised by a symbolic boundary based on ideas about gender equality, the need for integration and victimisation, challenges these women's aspirations and places them in a situation of (economic) dependency – on the goodwill of the husband abroad, on the economic resources of others and on their families. It also has a direct impact on the marriage system in Sri Lanka and on marriage conditions, to the disadvantage of women. These tests function as a means to filter the border in the country of origin. Doing this directly in the country of origin allows European countries to outsource governmentality as well as the costs of immigration.

Conclusion

This article has argued that jointly articulating the fields of bordering and boundary studies makes possible a nuanced understanding of current processes of differentiated exclusion. A symbolic boundary based on gendernationalism, integration and the victimisation of women legitimises a new governmentality of borders and a particular project of the politics of belonging.

The effects of this reconfigured border and boundary regime in the realm of marriage migration are considerable. First, this regime leads to a hierarchisation of marriage migrants and the exclusion of certain candidates. Similarly to what Gutekunst (2015) and (Jashari, Dahinden, & Moret, 2019) observed in Morocco and Turkey, respectively, this new border and boundary regime filters into Sri Lanka and affects would-be migrants according to their educational background and financial resources. Second, the externalisation of bordering practices directly impacts the spouses even before they migrate: it challenges their life aspirations, increases their economic dependency and precarity and has a direct impact on the marriage system. This case study has also demonstrated that the European vision of marriage is simultaneously ethnocentric, and, because of global inequalities and Western dominance, hegemonic.

Our analysis demonstrates how bordering and boundaries together make, rather than simply represent, a world, through political projects of governance and belonging. Policies restricting family reunification constitute a form of neo-colonial governance of borders and boundaries that reinforces global hierarchies that are historically anchored and ideologically constructed (Lutz, 1991; Nader, 1989). Pre-entry language tests allow European countries to externalise their borders, and thus to govern the cultural other before they have even left their country of origin.

Funding

This research project, entitled "Cross-border marriages under conditions of transnationalization and politicisation. A case study in Switzerland", was funded by the Swiss National Science Foundation (Grant 100017_149924). The publication of this article was also supported by the National Center of Competence in Research nccr – on the move, funded by the Swiss National Science Foundation (Grant 51NF40-142020).

Acknowledgements

We would like to warmly thank all the interview partners for having shared their intimate stories of marriage and their hopes and fears. Many thanks also to Chitra Russo for her valuable contribution and support as a translator in Sri Lanka. Earlier versions of this paper were presented on different occasions, and we would like to thank all those whose comments have helped improve the argument. Special thanks also to the external reviewers of Migration Letters, who helped sharpen the argument of the paper. Finally, we are grateful to Daniel Moure, who edited this article and rendered its language more elegant.

References

Amelina, A. (2017). Transnationalizing Inequalities in Europe. Sociocultural Boundaries, Assemblages and Regimes of Intersection. New York and London: Routledge.

Andrikopoulos, A. (2019). Love, money and papers in the affective circuits of cross-border marriages: beyond the 'sham'/'genuine' dichotomy. Journal of Ethnic and Migration Studies, 1-18. doi:10.1080/1369183X.2019.1625129

Barth, F. (1969). Introduction. In F. Barth (Ed.), Ethnic Groups and Boundaries: The Social Organization of Culture Difference (pp. 9-38). London: Allen & Unwin.

Block, L. (2014). Regulating Membership: Explaining Restriction and Stratification of Family Migration in Europe. Journal of Family Issues, doi: 10.1177/0192513X14557493.

Block, L. (2019). '(Im-)proper' members with '(im-)proper' families? – Framing spousal migration policies in Germany. Journal of Ethnic and Migration Studies, 1-18. doi:10.1080/1369183X.2019.1625132

Bonjour, S., & De Hart, B. (2013). A Proper Wife, a Proper Marriage: Construction.

Bonjour, S., & Kraler, A. (2014). Introduction: Family Migration as an Integration Issue? Policy Perspectives and Academic Insights. Journal of Family Issues, 1-26.

Carver, N. (2016). 'For her protection and benefit': the regulation of marriage-related migration to the UK. Ethnic and Racial Studies, 39(15), 2758-2776. doi:10.1080/01419870.2016.1171369

Charmaz, K. (2001). Qualitative Interviewing and Grounded Theory Analysis. In J. F. Gubrium & J. A. Holstein (Eds.), Handbook of Interview Research. Context and Methods (pp. 675-694). Thousand Oaks: Sage Publications.

Charsley, K., & Bolognani, M. (2019). Marrying 'in'/marrying 'out'? Blurred boundaries in British Pakistani marriage choices. Journal of Ethnic and Migration Studies, 1-18. doi:10.1080/1369183X.2019.1625131

Charsley, K., Bolognani, M., & Spencer, S. (2017). Marriage migration and integration: Interrogating assumptions in academic and policy debates. Ethnicities, 17(4), 469-490. doi:10.1177/1468796816677329

Dahinden, J., Fischer, C., Menet, J., & Kristol, A. (2018). Gendernationalism as a new Expression of Political Nationalism

De Genova, N. (2017). The Borders of "Europe" and the European Question. In N. De Genova (Ed.), The Borders of "Europe": Autonomy of Migration, Tactics of Bordering (pp. 1-35). Durham and London: Duke University Press.

Delphy, C. (2006). Antisexime ou antiracisme? Un faux dilemme. Nouvelles questions féministes, 25(1), 59-83.

Dietze, G. (2010). "Occidentalism", European Identity and Sexual Politics. In H. Brunkhorst & G. Grözinger (Eds.), The Study of Europe (pp. 87-116). Baden Baden: Nomos Verlag.

Eule, T., Borelli, L. M., Lindberg, A., & Wyss, A. (2018). Migrants Before the Law: Contested Migration Control in Europe: Springer.

Farris, S. R. (2017). Iin the Name of Women's Rights. The Rise of Femonationalism. Durham: Duke University Press.

Fassin, D. (2011). Policing Borders, Producing Boundaries. The Governmentality of Immigration in Dark Times. Annual Review of Anthropology, 40(213-26).

Favell, A. (2014). Immigration, Integration and Mobility: New Agendas in Migration Studies. Essays 1998–2014. Colchester: ECPR Press.

Gutekunst, M. (2015). Language as a new instrument of border control: the regulation of marriage migration from Morocco to Germany. The Journal of North African Studies, 20(4), 540-552. doi:10.1080/13629387.2015.1065038

Hadj Abdou, L. (2017). "Gender Nationalism": The New (Old) Politics of Belonging. OZP-Austrian Journal of Political Science, 46(1).

Jashari, S., Dahinden, J., & Moret, J. (2019). Alternative spatial hierarchies: a cross-border spouse's positioning strategies in the face of Germany's 'pre-integration' language test. Journal of Ethnic and Migration Studies, 1-17. doi:10.1080/1369183X.2019.1625136

Kolossov, V. (2005). Border Studies: Changing Perspectives and Theoretical Approaches. Geopolitics, 10(4), 606-632.

Korteweg, A., & Yudakul, G. (2009). Islam, Gender and Immigrant Integration: Boundary Drawing in Discourses on Honor Killing in the Netherlands and Germany. Ethnic and Racial Studies, 32(2), 218-238.

Lamont, M., & Molnar, V. (2002). The Study of Boundaries in the Social Sciences. Annual Review of Sociology, 28, 167-195.

Lavanchy, A. (2013). L'amour aux services de l'état civil : régulations institutionnelles de l'intimité et fabrique de la ressemblance nationale en Suisse. Migrations Société, 150, 61-77.

Lutz, H. (1991). The Mythe of the 'Other': Western Representation and Images of Migrant Women of so called 'Islamic Background'. International Review of Sociology, 2, 121-138.

Meuser, M., & Nagel, U. (2009). he Expert Interview and Changes in Knowledge Production. In A. Bogner, B. Littig, & W. Menz (Eds.), Interviewing Experts. Methodology and Practice (pp. 17-42). Basingstoke: Palgrave Mcmillan.

Mezzadra, S., & Neilson, B. (2012). Between Inclusion and Exclusion: On the Topology of Global Space and Borders. Theory, Culture & Society, 29(4/5), 58-78.

Moret, J., Andrikopoulos, A., & Dahinden, J. (2019). Contesting categories: cross-border marriages from the perspectives of the state, spouses and researchers. Journal of Ethnic and Migration Studies, 1-18. doi:10.1080/1369183X.2019.1625124

Nader, L. (1989). Orientalism, Occidentalism and the Control of Women. Cultural Dynamics, 2(3), 323-355.

Nieswand, B. (2018). Border dispositifs and border effects. Exploring the nexus between transnationalism and border studies. Identities, 25(5), 592-609. doi:10.1080/1070289X.2018.1507960

Paasi, A. (2011). A Border Theory: An Unattainable Dream or a Realistic Aim for Border Scholars? In D. Wastl-Walter (Ed.), The Ashgate Research Campanion to Border Studies (pp. 11-32). Farnham: Ashgate.

Pachucki, M. A., Pendergrass, S., & Lamont, M. (2007). Boundary Processes: Recent Theoretical Developments and New Contributions. Poetics, 35, 331-351.

Pellander, S. (2015). An Acceptable Marriage': Marriage Migration and Moral Gatekeeping in Finland. Journal of Family Issues, 36(11), 1472-1489.

Phillips, A. (2010). Gender & Culture. Cambridge: Polity Press.

Schinkel, W. (2018). Against 'Immigrant Integration': For an End to Neocolonial Knowledge Production. Comparative Migration Studies, 6(31).

Strasser, E., Kraler, A., Bonjour, S., & Bilger, V. (2009). Doing Family. Responses to the Constructions of the 'Migrant Family' across Europe. The History of the Family, 14, 165-176.

Strik, T., De Hart, B., & Nissen, E. (2013). Family Reunification: a barrier or facilitator of integration? A comparative study: Wolf Legal Publishers.

Swidler, A. (1986). Culture in Action: Symbols and Strategies. American Sociological Review, 51(2), 273-286.

Van Houtum, H. (2005). The Geopolitics of Borders and Boundaries. Geopolitics, 10(4), 672-679. doi:10.1080/14650040500318522

Van Houtum, H., & Van Naerssen, T. (2002). Bordering, Ordering and Othering. Tijdschrift voor economische en sociale geografie, 93(2), 125-136. doi:10.1111/1467-9663.00189

Walters, W. (2006). Border/Control. European Journal of Social Theory, 9(2), 187-203. doi:10.1177/1368431006063332

Wastl-Walter, D. (2012). The Ashgate Research Companion to Border Studies. Farnham: Ashgate.

Wilson, T. M., & Hastings, D. (2012). Borders and Border Studies. In T. M. Wilson & D. Hastings (Eds.), A Companion to Border Studies (pp. 1-25): Blackwell Publications Ltd.

Wimmer, A. (2002). Nationalist Exclusion and Ethnic Conflict. Shadows of Modernity. Cambridge: University Press.

Witzel, A., & Reiter, H. (2010). The Problem Centred Interview. Thousand Oaks: Sage Publication.

Wray, H., Agoston, A., & Hutton, J. (2014). A Family Resemblance? The Regulation of Marriage Migration in Europe. 16(2), 209. doi:https://doi.org/10.1163/15718166-12342054

Yuval-Davis, N. (2006). Belonging and the Politics of Belonging. Patterns of Prejudice(40), 197-214.

Yuval-Davis, N., Wemyss, G., & Cassidy, K. (2018). Everyday Bordering, Belonging and the Reorientation of British Immigration Legislation. Sociology, 52(2), 228-244. doi:10.1177/0038038517702599

Yuval-Davis, N., Wemyss, G., & Cassidy, K. (2019). Bordering. Cambridge: Polity Press.

July 2020
Volume: 17, **No**: 4, pp. 521 – 530
ISSN: 1741-8984
e-ISSN: 1741-8992
www.migrationletters.com

MIGRATION
LETTERS

First Submitted: 1 February 2019 Accepted: 27 August 2019
DOI: https://doi.org/10.33182/ml.v17i4.692

(Re)producing Boundaries While Enforcing Borders in Immigration Detention

Laura Rezzonico[1]

Abstract

Immigration detention centres can be conceptualised as sites of bordering that separate the wanted from the unwanted and reify the boundary between citizens and non-citizens. Using boundary making as an analytical lens that allows getting insights into the work of borders, this paper addresses the relationship between staff and detainees in these ambiguous sites, asking how staff members engage in boundary work to distance themselves from the pains of detainees and to legitimise their work in an institution of exclusion. It considers boundary making based on three kinds of categories – race, ethnicity and culture; (il)legality and (un)deservingness; and unknownness and criminality – that are morally charged. Through the construction of detainees as culturally and morally different, illegal and undeserving, as well as potentially dangerous, prison staff contribute to the reinforcement of borders, legitimating their exclusionary dimension.

Keywords: *Immigrant detention; exclusion; borders; boundaries; deservingness.*

Introduction

Since the 1990s, immigration detention has become a normalised instrument of states' "arsenals of [migration] control" (Bloch & Schuster, 2005: 508). Switzerland is no exception, and every year approximately 3,000-5,000 migrants[2] are confined – most of the time in ordinary prisons – with the aim of facilitating their deportation[3]. Immigration detention[4] – the holding of foreign nationals for purposes related to immigration enforcement – can be conceptualised as a practice of bordering (Mountz et al., 2013), separating the wanted from the unwanted (van Houtum, 2010) and reifying the boundary between citizens and non-citizens (Griffiths, 2013). In this article, I use boundary making (Wimmer, 2013) as an analytical lens that allows insights into the work of borders, showing how categories of inclusion and exclusion are (re)produced – while also contested – at the border. Indeed, as closed spaces in which different actors of the border regime come into contact, detention facilities happen to be privileged sites for understanding the mutual relationship that exists between processes of bordering and boundary making (Fassin, 2011).

Detention centres produce high levels of suffering for detainees, whose experiences are characterised by detriment (Moran et al., 2018), uncertainty (Bosworth, 2014; Griffiths, 2013; Turnbull, 2016), and overwhelming feelings of injustice (Bosworth, 2013; Campesi, 2015; Lietaert

---

[1] Laura Rezzonico, former member of the NCCR on the move, Centre de droit des migrations, Laboratoire d'études des processus sociaux, Université de Neuchâtel, Rue Abram-Louis Breguet 1, CH-2000 Neuchâtel, Switzerland. E-mail: laura.rezzonico@unine.ch.

[2] According to the State Secretariat for Migration, 5,732 detention orders were issued in 2016 (year of my research). Since then, there has been a decrease in numbers of detention orders: 3,724 in 2017; 3,284 in 2018; and 2,921 in 2019 (SEM, 2018; 2020). Between 2011 and 2017, 92% of detained migrants were men, and two thirds were (mainly rejected) asylum seekers (Achermann et al., 2019).

[3] Immigration detention can be ordered by Swiss cantons against non-citizens with the aim of identification and/or ensuring the enforcement of their removal from national territory, and can last up to 18 months (Foreign Nationals and Integration Act, Art. 73 to 82).

[4] In the following pages, when not specified, "detention" refers to "immigration detention".

et al., 2014). With their high emotional charge, institutions of confinement are also difficult working places. According to Bosworth (2013), they display a legitimacy deficit which causes confusion and uncertainty for staff members, who do not dispose of the same sources of legitimacy as prison officers. In this context, staff members engage in legitimation work, using narrative techniques that "construct their activities as justified, rational, and legitimate" (Ugelvik, 2016: 216).

To avoid being overwhelmed with suffering, detention staff develop psychological techniques of estrangement and detachment as a form of self-care (Gill, 2016). The concept of moral distance, as developed by Gill (2016: 4), is particularly useful to understand these processes. It refers to the "the human tendency to care more for people close to us than to those far away", where distance is not only geographical: indifference does not always derive from remoteness and unfamiliarity, but can also emerge in situations of sustained contact and overfamiliarity, such as in detention centres.

In this article, I look precisely into *how* staff members distance themselves from detainees through the construction and reproduction of boundaries, a process that is also fostered by institutional features. Using boundary work as an analytical lens to study the perspective of staff members allows me to show how they cope with and make sense of their work in immigration detention through the production and maintenance of moral boundaries. This boundary making, I argue, serves two purposes: distancing themselves from the pains of detainees, and legitimising their own work in an institution of exclusion. Through the construction of detainees as culturally and morally different, illegal and undeserving, as well as potentially dangerous, prison staff contribute to the reinforcement of borders, legitimating their exclusionary dimension.

In order to make this point, I start by introducing the concept of boundaries and their relation to morality in the next section. After a short description of my fieldwork, I describe the context of interactions between staff and detainees and the institutional aspects that impact on them. I then go through three different kinds of boundary making based on categories of: 1) race, ethnicity and culture; 2) (il)legality and (un)deservingness; and 3) unknownness and criminality, to show how these are morally charged and ultimately serve to legitimise immigration detention.

Boundaries and their moral dimension

In the light of Barth's (1969) work on ethnicity, academics have focused on how boundaries work to construct and maintain social difference. Some have focused on immigration societies, showing that *boundary making* involves actors from the majority *and* the minority, "creating both immigrant minorities and national majorities in the process" (Wimmer, 2009: 245). Boundaries are intimately related to power and inequality, which is at best captured by the distinction introduced by Lamont and Molnár (2002: 168) between symbolic boundaries as categorisations made by social actors and social boundaries as "objectified forms of social differences manifested in unequal access to and unequal distribution of resources (...) and social opportunities". Social actors thus engage in struggles over which boundaries should be considered relevant (Wimmer, 2013).

Moral categories and values are central to boundary making (Barth, 1969; Pachucki et al., 2007), particularly when it comes to defining and legitimising the boundaries of citizenship and belonging through notions of deservingness (Chauvin and Garcés-Mascareñas, 2012). Distinct from the discourse of rights, which presumes universality and equality before the law, deservingness is articulated in a moral register based on a specific circumstance (Willen, 2012: 813-814). It has been argued, however, that access to rights has been re-moralised in the context of the 'war on terror', becoming connected to the perceived moral value of a person (Eckert, 2008). Through a process of *othering*, societies construct the enemy as external while reproducing the dichotomy of 'us' and 'them' that underlies what Eckert calls a 'dual law' system.

In the context of migration politics, Chauvin and Garcés-Mascareñas (2012: 247) use the concept of the "moral economy of illegality"[5] to refer to "the discourse–policy nexus regulating the construction of irregular migrants as more or less illegal" on moral grounds. Focusing on the tension between framings of unauthorised migrants as civic culprits to be punished and civic minors who deserve membership, the authors show how such boundaries between the *good* and *bad* 'illegal' allow states to exert disciplinary power over undocumented migrants. In this paper, I look into how moral categories construct detainees as more or less estimable and deserving. I use the term 'moral categories' to refer to those categorisations based on perceptions and ideas of 'good' and 'bad', 'right' and 'wrong', and thus operating through a judgement of value.

About this research

This article is based on ethnographic data collected for my doctoral thesis[6] between 2015 and 2017 in two Swiss prisons confining migrants awaiting deportation along with (although separated from) remand and/or convicted criminals. This is a normalised practice in Switzerland, where most facilities used for immigration detention are ordinary prisons[7]. The two facilities are located in the German-speaking part of Switzerland, each providing for approximately 70 to 150 detention places. One is a male prison that hires exclusively male officers, while the other comprises a small female section[8] and employs approximately one-third female staff. In this latter facility – not intended for long detention periods – at the time of my fieldwork male detainees were locked up between 19 and 23 hours per day depending on the cell they were assigned to; they had one hour walk daily but no work or leisure activities; and they could receive only three hours visit per week. In the male-only facility, conditions were slightly more lenient, with the opportunity to work a few hours a day, to access the courtyard three hours a day, and to receive visits up to 12 hours a week.

In both prisons, I conducted participant observation, shadowing the staff in their daily work, and in the male-only facility, I also joined detainees' daily walks during several months. Despite my interviewees comprising detainees and others attending the prison space, this article is mostly based on 21 interviews conducted with staff members of the two prisons and informal conversations held during participant observation. Staff members had been informed of my visits through the circulation of information sheets describing the research aims and methods[9]. Interviews took place during working hours and on a voluntary basis: staff members could sign up for an interview, although I directly proposed interviews to some with whom I had good personal contact.

---

[5] The authors draw on Fassin's (2009) concept of "moral economy" intended as the production, circulation and use of moral sentiments, emotions, values and norms in the social space.

[6] The doctoral research was carried out within the framework of a larger project entitled "Restricting Immigration: Practices, Experiences and Resistance", directed by Prof. Christin Achermann at the University of Neuchâtel, and part of the National Centre of Competence in Research nccr – on the move, financed by the Swiss National Science Foundation.

[7] The infrastructure of immigration detention in Switzerland is heterogeneous, with more than 30 facilities scattered across the national territory providing for approximately 500 detainees. Of these, only five are used exclusively for immigration detention, while the others operate several detention regimes at a time. This occurs despite the law stating that detention shall take place in dedicated facilities and separately from persons in pre-trial detention or who are serving a criminal sentence (FNIA, Art. 81).

[8] As the female section was empty during my fieldwork, I could not conduct participant observation there or interview any female detainees.

[9] For detainees, information sheets in several languages were hung in the detention area in the prison where I conducted most participant observation. In the other facility, I provided forms to sign up for interviews (including information on the research) that were circulated a couple of times among detainees.

Physical and institutional boundaries in detention centres

In order to discuss boundary work in detention facilities, it is important to situate interactions and characterise the relations between staff and detainees. Those are significantly shaped by the material and institutional context of the prison, which works to avoid meaningful encounters – intended as "morally obligating interactions" – and create distance between the two groups (Gill, 2016: 80). Here, I will address three main institutional features that shape this relation and the construction of boundaries: architecture, organisational concerns and the roles assigned to staff and detainees by the institution.

First, the architectural and spatial configuration of the prison contributes to shaping the relationships and distinctions between staff and detainees (Kynsilehto & Puumala, 2017: 209), while spatial arrangements influence interactions (see Enjolras, 2010). A tangible example was found in one of the two prisons observed, where most interactions occurred through a porthole in the door, hiding the body of the interlocutors from integral view, thus hindering effective communication and fostering processes of dehumanisation (see Bhui, 2013).

Along with such physical barriers, organisational measures contribute to creating distance between staff and detainees. For example, the rotation of staff around the prison obstructs the establishment of personal relationships with detainees, given their relatively high turnover, and acts as a powerful mechanism facilitating the detachment of staff from individual pains of detainees (see Gill, 2016), a function that is valued by prison management. The need to complete a form to make requests is another example of such measures that, despite being motivated by efficiency, mediates communication while establishing a distance between staff and detainees.

Third, interpersonal relationships in detention facilities are clearly influenced by the roles attributed to detainees and staff by the prison. For Goffman (1961: 111), "staging a difference between two constructed categories of persons – a difference in social quality and moral character, a difference in perceptions of self and other" is one of the main accomplishments of 'total institutions' such as the prison. For example, the uniform worn by officers symbolises their controlling role, differentiating them from detainees. This asymmetry in appearance mirrors the asymmetry in power: detainees are dependent on staff for movement, food, medical care, etc. while prison staff have the power to lock doors and, under certain circumstances, sanction detainees. Prison officers are supposed both to control and assist detainees while following strict rules and maintaining a 'professional' relationship. This requires avoiding any personal involvement in individual cases, a task that is facilitated by the fragmentation of the deportation system. Indeed, the prison has no other role than to hold detainees and keep them at the disposal of migration authorities, which means that prison officers know very little about the individual situations of detainees, while decision-makers are kept distant from detainees (see also Bosworth, 2014; Gill, 2016).

Boundary making based on race, ethnicity and culture

In the context just described, I argue that staff members make sense of their role through the drawing and maintenance of different kinds of boundaries. A first type is based on categories of race, ethnicity, religion and culture, which represent a tempting explanation for the different behaviours observed among detainees (see Bosworth & Slade, 2014). Staff members often base their discourses and ways of handling detainees on stereotypes or previous experience with inmates of the same geographic origin. It is quite common to hear stereotyped, and sometimes racist statements like "North Africans are aggressive and arrogant" or "Black Africans are easy, you give them food, and they are happy" (fieldnotes), particularly during informal conversations. These ethnicised and racialised representations of detainees sometimes have a moral dimension, as in this quotation implying that people from North Africa would have a cultural inclination for crime:

"(…) basically, the law doesn't interest them [detainees from North African countries] at all. (…) There are many who (...) have stolen something, whether it's a mobile phone, or a laptop (...). They take everything, right? And if you talk to them and ask them why they stole, [they answer] 'that's how it works at our place [in our country]'" (Dario, prison officer)[10].

Similarly, gender equality is also mobilised in some discourses as 'cultural stuff' to construct detainees as different and morally dubious (Duemmler et al., 2010), inferring that they – particularly 'Arabs', a general term used for citizens of the Maghreb and other countries with Arab and/or Muslim majority – are disrespectful towards female officers and women in general, while gender equality is presented as a value and an achievement of Swiss, or Western, society.

The introduction of racial and cultural boundaries *between* different groups of migrants reinforces the institutional boundary between staff and detainees, constructing the detainee as non-belonging to 'us' and unassimilable. In this vein, ethnic minority staff are sometimes considered exceptional examples of integration, which paradoxically reinforces that boundary[11]. For those staff members, however, their position requires them to further distance themselves from detainees and show loyalty to the institution, as described here:

"At the beginning it was pretty difficult, because they [detainees from the same origin] take advantage of you, they have the feeling you belong to them, not… Then setting boundaries is important, showing them, stop, I get not paid from you, I get paid from this side" (Ivan, prison officer).

Boundaries between employees and detainees, then, are not only a matter of ethno-cultural or national belonging, but have a clear institutional dimension, which requires staff members to resort to other categories of difference.

Boundary making based on categories of illegality and deservingness

Besides ethnic and racial categories, legal and administrative categories are powerful markers of social difference in the boundary work done by staff in order to make sense of immigration detention, and again they have an important moral dimension. In particular, staff members understand detention through the lens of 'illegality', despite being aware that immigration detainees are not incarcerated for a criminal offence: "they are not criminals, but… they are still illegal", they argue. Rather than being acknowledged as a consequence of a restrictive system, 'illegality' is often seen as a consequence of people's bad choices and/or morality. Furthermore, this notion establishes an analogy with prisoners, who are held for breaking the law, which produces ambiguity and confusion among staff members (Bosworth, 2014).

It has been argued, however, that 'illegality' does not automatically function as "an absolute marker of illegitimacy" (Chauvin and Garcés-Mascareñas, 2012: 243), where an emerging "moral

[10] Translations from German are from the author, while employees' names have been changed for anonymity.
[11] See Tassin (2016) for a thorough analysis of the dynamics of categorisation and hierarchisation within the staff.

526 (Re)producing Boundaries While Enforcing Borders in Immigration Detention

economy of deservingness" introduces different grades of (il)legality (Chauvin and Garcés-Mascareñas, 2014). In the case under scrutiny, this moral economy is highly influenced by the institutional context of detention: on one hand, being confined in a penitentiary works to delegitimise migrants through their symbolic criminalisation; on the other hand, the imagination of detention as coming at the end of a probatory path through which they have to prove their need for protection and/or their civic value contributes to moralised perceptions of undeservingness.

Indeed, detention is mainly understood within a state system which sorts 'true' refugees from 'bogus' asylum seekers and legitimate from illegitimate migrants (see Darley, 2010). As a result, those who end up in detention must inevitably be the 'undeserving' ones:

"I think that we live in a state under the rule of law [Rechtsstaat]! (…) they have so many rights and particularly we [emphasis] in Switzerland, we take extreme care that it [the country of deportation] is not a country where someone is persecuted, that it is not a country where there is war. (…) I assume that they [the detainees] are of two sorts: economic refugees and criminals who are worried about a criminal prosecution at home" (Peter, prison officer).

For this employee, deportation comes at the end of a procedure that allocates a status to those who deserve it. Firmly believing in the Swiss system and highlighting the supposed fairness and generosity of the state with migrants in general, detention is then seen as a 'necessary evil' to cope with the abuses of that system:

"Something that always depresses me is that many people from Syria are shown on TV, how they have to sleep under tents – old people, children, and so on. They are not here, because here are… many young people, who have money, who partly have done (…) 'big shit', they are here. The poor people who are down there, they cannot come, because they don't have the money for the journey. That's the worst [thing]" (Dario, prison officer).

According to this officer, people who are in real need of protection are too destitute and helpless to undertake the journey to Europe. This depoliticised image of the 'genuine refugee' as a suffering victim fleeing from persecution is counterposed to the figure of the 'bogus asylum seeker', usually imagined as male, young, black and/or Muslim, who does not deserve compassion or protection. This dichotomy has a strong gender dimension: the feminisation of the image of the refugee as a passive victim results in the demonisation of rejected male asylum seekers, who in opposition are seen as excessively agentive and opportunistic, lying and trying to abuse the system (Griffiths, 2015; Scheel and Squire, 2014). Symbolically, the fact of being held in prison amplifies this representation of detainees as lacking a sense of morality.

If actual need and responsibility for it intervene in the moral evaluation of deservingness, so do attitudes towards support in the form of docility and gratefulness (Oorschot, 2000). When detainees do not comply with the expectation of being docile, passive and dependent (Griffiths, 2015), they display a 'lack of gratitude' in the eyes of some employees, which is seen as evidence of their immorality and 'inauthenticity' (Hall, 2012; see also Darley, 2010 on the relation between gratitude and deservingness):

"(…) the gratitude [emphasis]… they are safe now. They have fled from war, from famine, and then the trash is so full with food leftovers! That is questionable as well, because the tap is running all the time… [In your country] you do not have the resources, you have to walk a few kilometres to the water and it is scarce, and here you let the water run, because it comes from the wall, right? That's what I don't understand" (Jan, prison officer).

Besides being contradictory in its reference to safety, this quotation implies that detainees should be grateful, reflecting their representation as (illegal and undesired) *guests* (Hall, 2010). Illegality and ungratefulness are used as markers of difference that create a moral boundary not only between citizens and non-citizens, but also between deserving and undeserving guests, the latter forming a powerful category of exclusion.

'Unknown' identity as a threat

If cultural, legal and moral categories are used to construct the detainee as different and undeserving, another element is categorisation as 'the unknown'. Identity becomes particularly salient in detention as revealing it and/or providing identity documents can result in quick deportation. Consequently, states make considerable efforts to fix the identities of migrants (Mountz et al., 2013), who sometimes attempt to resist them. The resulting contested or 'unknown' identities make detainees unreliable and potentially dangerous in the eyes of prison staff (see also Griffiths, 2014; Hall, 2010). A prison officer used the metaphor "walking in the darkness" to describe working in immigration detention, pointing to insecurity felt because of unknown identities, resulting in lower capacity for trust (see also Bosworth, 2014: 183; Hall, 2010).

This unknown character leaves space for imagination: "The problem is, you don't know who they are, they could have killed ten people in their country of origin and ten during their journey to Europe, or they could be rapists, or they could have done nothing bad, you just don't know" (informal conversation). Despite being held for a migration enforcement goal, detainees become suspects of crime because of their unknown identity and past. This is reinforced by the presence of certain migrants with criminal records placed alongside immigration detainees, and even more by the institutional context of the prison, characterised by a co-presence of immigration and penal detainees, held in almost identical conditions.

The construction of detained migrants as potentially criminal reflects gendered and racialised representations of criminality that are reinforced through the symbolic use of the prison as a space of punishment. The fact that statistically, the population of immigration detainees shares several characteristics with the population of the criminal justice system – being predominantly male, young and of foreign nationality – contributes to blurring the categories[12]. Furthermore, detainees' outbursts of rage and despair can sometimes result in aggressive behaviours (towards others or themselves) and are discursively used by staff to sustain their potential dangerousness.

The construction of detainees as threatening justifies a series of security measures based on pre-emption and hypervigilance (Hall, 2010, 2012) as well as the use of physical force for control. Furthermore, it helps staff to rationalise feelings of fear that are taboo in prison work as considered too 'feminine' (Crawley & Crawley, 2008), turning detainees into an objective danger. Indeed, both discourses presenting detainees as dangerous and practices to control and restrain them contribute to the construction of prison work as a male job. Through the display of strength and vigour, staff members assert their masculinity (see Tassin, 2016; Hall, 2012), compensating for the frustration

---

[12] Men represent approximately 92% of immigration detainees and 94% of prisoners; the average age is respectively 29 and 34; and the rate of foreign national penal inmates reaches 68% (calculated on the basis of data published by the Swiss Federal Statistical Office for 2019 on the population of incarcerated people).

that the perceived feminine nature of many of their tasks – such as delivering food or laundry – produce.

This criminalising discourse tends to present detainees as enemies or 'villains' through the making of a moral boundary that ultimately serves to legitimise the work and practices of immigration detention (Ugelvik, 2016), as well as the existence of a parallel system – a 'law for enemies' (Eckert, 2008) – that does not provide the same rights as it does for citizens.

Conclusion

We have seen how prison staff create boundaries between themselves and detainees through categories of culture and race, legality and deservingness, unknown identity and dangerousness. These boundaries work to legitimate their role in the deportation system as well as to facilitate moral distancing from inmates and their suffering (Gill, 2016). The emotional weight of boundary work for prison officers would be an interesting focus for further research. An intersectional analysis of detention centres would also benefit from research in female or mixed institutions, where gender categories would arise more explicitly in the boundary work of staff.

Despite this not being the focus of the article, it is important to highlight that detainees clearly contest the legitimacy of their incarceration, questioning the categories through which they are othered, and inverting moral arguments to highlight the immoral character of immigration detention. In this way, detention centres become the stage of boundary work based on morality, at the same time, constitutive of struggles between actors of the border regime (Casas-Cortes et al., 2015). Further research could shed light on such border struggles, focusing not only on how practices of border enforcement reproduce national boundaries but also on how those are contested and challenged by several actors.

In this article, I have shown how the organisation of immigration detention in carceral institutions that are part of the criminal justice system blurs the distinction between illegality and criminality, which helps legitimise migrants' exclusion. The prison as a space of punishment affixes categories of criminality and immorality onto migrant detainees, which are reproduced in staff members' discourses. Intensive boundary work is needed to justify a system that deprives migrants of the right to liberty for administrative reasons, in the same institutions as prisoners who are punished for a criminal offence. Through the construction of boundaries that are morally charged, staff members legitimise detention as a practice of border enforcement that aims at excluding non-members while reaffirming the normative boundaries of national membership that institutionalise and reproduce global inequality.

References

Achermann, C., Bertrand, A.-L., Miaz, J., & Rezzonico, L. (2019). *Administrative detention of foreign nationals in figures*. Policy briefs "in a nutshell", 12. Neuchâtel: nccr – on the move. https://nccr-onthemove.ch/knowledge-transfer/policy-briefs/administrative-detention-of-foreign-nationals-in-figures/

Barth, F. (1969). *Ethnic groups and boundaries: The social organisation of culture difference*. Boston: Little, Brown and Company.

Bhui, H. S. (2013). "Introduction: Humanising migration control and detention". In: K. F. Aas & M. Bosworth (eds.), *The Borders of Punishment: Migration, Citizenship, and Social Exclusion*, 1-17, Oxford: Oxford University Press.

Bloch, A., & Schuster, L. (2005). "At the extremes of exclusion: Deportation, detention and dispersal". *Ethnic and Racial Studies*, 28 (3): 491-512. https://doi.org/10.1080/0141987042000337858

Bosworth, M. (2013). "Can Immigration Detention Centres be Legitimate? Understanding Confinement in a Global World". In: K. Aas and M. Bosworth (eds.), *The Borders of Punishment: Migration, Citizenship, and Social Exclusion*, 151-165, Oxford: Oxford University Press.

Bosworth, M. (2014). *Inside immigration detention*. Oxford: Oxford Univesity Press.

Bosworth, M., & Slade, G. (2014). "In search of recognition: Gender and staff–detainee relations in a British immigration removal centre". *Punishment & Society,* 16 (2): 169-186. https://doi.org/10.1177/1462474513517017

Campesi, G. (2015). "Hindering the deportation machine: An ethnography of power and resistance in immigration detention." *Punishment & Society-International Journal of Penology*, 17 (4): 427-453. https://doi.org/10.1177/1462474515603804

Chauvin, S. and Garcés-Mascareñas, B. (2014). "Becoming Less Illegal: Deservingness Frames and Undocumented Migrant Incorporation." *Sociology Compass*, 8 (4): 422-432. https://doi.org/10.1111/soc4.12145

Chauvin, S. and Garcés-Mascareñas, B. (2012). "Beyond Informal Citizenship: The New Moral Economy of Migrant Illegality." *International Political Sociology*, 6 (3): 241-259. https://hdl.handle.net/11245/1.374747

Casas-Cortes, M., Cobarrubias, S., De Genova, N., Garelli, G., Grappi, G., Heller, C., ... Tazzioli, M. (2015). "New Keywords: Migration and Borders". *Cultural Studies*, 29 (1): 55-87. https://doi.org/10.1080/09502386.2014.891630

Crawley, E., & Crawley, P. (2008). "Understanding prison officers: Culture, cohesion and conflict". In: J. Bennett, B. Crewe, & A. Wahidin (eds.), *Understanding prison staff*, 134-152, Cullompton, UK ; Portland, Or.: Willan Pub.

Darley, M. (2010). "Le pouvoir de la norme. La production du jugement et son contournement dans les lieux d'enfermement des étrangers". *Déviance et Société*, 34 (2): 229-239. https://doi.org/10.3917/ds.342.0229

Duemmler, K., Dahinden, J., & Moret, J. (2010). "Gender equality as 'cultural stuff': Ethnic boundary work in a classroom in Switzerland". *Diversities,* 12 (1): 21-39. http://doc.rero.ch/record/20723

Eckert, Julia (2008). "Laws for Enemies". In: Eckert, J.M. (ed.), *The social life of anti-terrorism laws: the war on terror and the classifications of the "dangerous other"*, 7-32, Bielefeld: transcript.

Enjolras, F. (2010). "Des policiers aux frontières: La gestion ordinaire d'un centre de rétention". In: D. Fassin (ed.), *Les nouvelles frontières de la société française*, 219-243, Paris: La Découverte.

Fassin, D. (2009). "Les économies morales revisitées". *Annales. Histoire, Sciences Sociales*, 64e année (6): 1237-1266. https://www.cairn.info/revue-annales-2009-6-page-1237.htm

Fassin, D. (2011). "Policing borders, producing boundaries. The governmentality of immigration in dark times". *Annual Review of Anthropology*, 40: 213-226. https://doi.org/10.1146/annurev-anthro-081309-145847

Gill, N. (2016). *Nothing personal?: Geographies of governing and activism in the British asylum system*. John Wiley & Sons.

Goffman, E. (1961). *Asylums: Essays on the social situation of mental patients and other inmates*. New York: Anchor books.

Griffiths, M. (2013). "Living with uncertainty: Indefinite immigration detention". *Journal of Legal Anthropology*, 1 (3): 263-286. https://doi.org/10.3167/jla.2013.010301

Griffiths, M. (2014). "Men and the emotional world of immigration detention". In B. Anderson & M. Keith (eds.), *Migration: A COMPAS Anthology [Online]. https://compasanthology.co.uk/men-emotional-world-immigration-detention/*

Griffiths, M. (2015). "'Here, man is nothing!': Gender and policy in an asylum context". *Men and Masculinities*, 18 (4): 468-488. https://doi.org/10.1177/1097184X15575111

Hall, A. (2010). "'These people could be anyone': Fear, contempt (and empathy) in a British immigration removal centre". *Journal of Ethnic and Migration Studies*, 36 (6): 881-898. https://doi.org/10.1080/13691831003643330

Hall, A. (2012). *Border watch: Cultures of immigration, detention and control*. London; New York: Pluto Press.

Kynsilehto, A., & Puumala, E. (2017). "Intimate economies of state practice: Materialities of detention in Finland". In: D. Conlon & N. Hiemstra (eds.), *Intimate economies of immigration detention: critical perspectives*, 203-218, Abingdon: Routledge.

Lamont, M. and Molnár, V. (2002). "The study of boundaries in the social sciences". *Annual Review of Sociology*, 28: 167-195. https://www.jstor.org/stable/3069239

Lietaert, I., Broekaert, E. and Derluyn, I. (2014). "The Lived Experiences of Migrants in Detention." *Population, Space and Place*, 21 (6): 568-579. https://doi.org/10.1002/psp.1861

Moran, D., Turner, J. and Schliehe, A.K. (2018). "Conceptualising the carceral in carceral geography". *Progress in Human Geography*, 42 (5): 666–686. https://doi.org/10.1177/0309132517710352

Mountz, A., Coddington, K., Catania, R. T., & Loyd, J. M. (2013). "Conceptualising detention: Mobility, containment, bordering, and exclusion". *Progress in Human Geography*, 37 (4): 522-541. https://doi.org/10.1177/0309132512460903

Oorschot, W. van (2000). "Who should get what, and why? On deservingness criteria and the conditionality of solidarity among the public". *Policy & Politics*, 28 (1): 33-48. https://doi.org/10.1332/0305573002500811

Pachucki, M. A., Pendergrass, S. and Lamont, M. (2007). "Boundary processes: Recent theoretical developments and new contributions". *Poetics*, 35 (6): 331-351. https://doi.org/10.1016/j.poetic.2007.10.001

Scheel, S, and Squire, V. (2014). "Forced migrants as 'illegal' migrants". In: E. Fiddian-Qasmiyeh et al. (eds.), *The Oxford handbook of refugee and forced migration studies*, Oxford: Oxford University Press.

SEM (2018). *Rapport sur la migration 2017*. Secrétariat d'État aux Migrations, Bern. https://www.sem.admin.ch/dam/data/sem/publiservice/berichte/migration/migrationsbericht-2017-f.pdf

SEM (2020). *Rapport sur la migration 2019*. Secrétariat d'État aux Migrations, Bern. https://www.sem.admin.ch/dam/sem/fr/data/publiservice/berichte/migration/migrationsbericht-2019-f.pdf.download.pdf/migrationsbericht-2019-f.pdf

Tassin, L. (2016). "Les frontières de la rétention: Genre et ethnicité dans le contrôle des étrangers en instance d'expulsion". *Critique internationale*, 72 (3): 35-52. https://doi.org/10.3917/crii.072.0035

Turnbull, S. (2016). "'Stuck in the middle': Waiting and uncertainty in immigration detention". *Time & Society*, 25 (1), 61–79. https://doi.org/10.1177/0961463X15604518

Ugelvik, T. (2016). "Techniques of legitimation: The narrative construction of legitimacy among immigration detention officers". *Crime, Media, Culture*, 12(2): 215-232.

van Houtum, H. (2010). "Human blacklisting: The global apartheid of the EU's external border regime". *Environment and Planning D: Society and Space*, 28 (6): 957-976. https://doi.org/10.1068/d1909

Willen, S. (2012). "How is health-related "deservingness" reckoned? Perspectives from unauthorised im/migrants in Tel Aviv". *Social Science & Medicine*, 74 (6): 812-821. https://doi.org/10.1016/j.socscimed.2011.06.033

Wimmer, A. (2009). "Herder's Heritage and the Boundary-Making Approach: Studying Ethnicity in Immigrant Societies". *Sociological Theory*, 27 (3): 244-270. https://doi.org/10.1111/j.1467-9558.2009.01347.x

Wimmer, A. (2013). *Ethnic boundary making: Institutions, power, networks*. Oxford: Oxford University Press.

July 2020
Volume: 17, **No**: 4, pp. 531 – 540
ISSN: 1741-8984
e-ISSN: 1741-8992
www.migrationletters.com

MIGRATION
LETTERS

First Submitted: 16 August 2019 Accepted: 1 April 2020
DOI: https://doi.org/10.33182/ml.v17i4.836

Manifestations and Contestations of Borders and Boundaries in Everyday Understandings of Integration

Carolin Fischer[1]

Abstract

This article asks how borders and boundaries manifest themselves in understandings of integration. Drawing on qualitative interviews with migrant descendants living in Zürich, Switzerland, it investigates how understandings of integration are experienced, interpreted, appropriated and modified, in relation to either the self or others. I employ de Certeau's theory of the practice of everyday life to establish how borders and boundaries are reflected in individual meaning-making, perceptions of self and other and the ways in which people situate themselves in society. I demonstrate not only that the interplay between borders and boundaries informs specific aspects of migration governance such as integration policies, but also that people employ tactics based on enunciations of integration to act upon the social position they are allocated as a result of ascribed, racialised markers of difference.

Keywords: *borders; boundaries; practice of everyday life; integration.*

Introduction

Nation-state borders play an important role in shaping forms, experiences and the governance of human mobility. In conjunction with global social inequalities, borders – in terms of migration policies, laws and regulations – define legal subjects (Fassin, 2020) and filter people's mobility (Bauder, 2017; Bakewell, 2008). Borders thus 'react to diverse kinds of migrant subjectivities and thereby operate to produce differentiated forms of access and "rights"' (Casas-Cortes et al., 2015: 57). As a result, migrants face different restrictions and enjoy different entitlements when seeking to cross borders and upon arrival at a destination. However, nation-state borders also delineate bounded and imagined communities (Anderson, 1983). Administratively, citizenship determines an individual's entitlements and restrictions in a given national context. It is also a marker of a symbolic distinction between inside and outside, us and them, foreign and familiar. People are assigned specific attributes on the basis of their place of origin. It is here that borders and boundaries coincide. As social constructs, boundaries establish symbolic differences between, for example, classes, gender, race and religion, and they produce identifications based on these classification markers. Boundaries thus separate people into groups, which foster feelings of similarity, membership and belonging (Lamont and Molnár, 2002). They can be mobilised to distinguish between those accepted as members and those classified as undesirable residents of the national territory.

The territorial fixing of borders contributes to the making of others. Borders thus impose their presence on both social relations and individual identification, for which boundary work is an

---
[1] Carolin Fischer, Ambizione Research Fellow, University of Bern, Institute of Social Anthropology, Lerchenweg 36, 3012 Bern, Switzerland. E-mail: carolin.fischer@anthro.unibe.ch.

essential element (Anderson, 2019; Amelina, 2017; Dahinden, 2016; Wimmer, 2008). As a result, migration involves constant processes of reinvention and self-definition among both migrants and the societies they enter (see van Houtum and van Naerssen, 2002). Such boundaries between migrants and those perceived as native citizens often extend across generations and continue to affect people and groups who are not migrants themselves (Dahinden et al., forthcoming; Dahinden et al., 2014). Recent debates about the emergence of 'parallel societies' in different European contexts (Bukow et al., 2007) exemplify how political and public discourses build on ideas of lasting otherness. That migrants and their descendants embody the articulation of borders and boundaries is now well established in migration studies and beyond (Fassin, 2005; Kearney, 1991). However, it is far from clear how and where the interlocking logics of inclusion, exclusion and distinction manifest themselves. Who exactly do they affect, under what circumstances and with what effects? So far, little attention has been paid to the articulations and consequences of the interplay between borders and boundaries at the level of individual meaning-making.

To understand how borders and boundaries coincide in people's everyday lives, I examine the normative principle and politics of migrant integration. More specifically, I uncover how descendants of migrants mobilise understandings of integration to describe their experiences and sense of belonging or non-belonging to society. Drawing on qualitative interview data that were generated in Zürich, Switzerland, I investigate how people who were born and raised in immigrant families experience, interpret, appropriate and modify understandings of integration, in relation to either themselves or perceived others. I explore how the interplay of borders and boundaries affects individual meaning-making, perceptions of self and other and the ways in which people situate themselves in society. To this end, I employ de Certeau's theory of the practice of everyday life to identify different understandings of the term 'integration'. These understandings, I argue, reflect people's positions in the interplay of borders and boundaries as well as the tactics they apply to manipulate these positions. First, however, I reflect on how the idea and politics of integration exemplify the coincidence of borders and boundaries.

Exploring the interplay of borders and boundaries through understandings of integration

'Integration' is a fuzzy concept with multiple definitions (Grillo, 2003), but common to all of them is that they produce and reproduce specific ideas of society, the state, the nation and the relationship between majorities and minorities. Integration is hence best described as a social imaginary (Rytter, 2019; Taylor, 2004) that is inextricably tied to the bounded territory of the modern nation-state. Indeed, '[t]he making of a unique, exclusive place goes hand in hand with governing practices of exclusion and purification' (van Houtum and van Naerssen, 2002: 127). Through borders and the ways in which borders, the bounded territory and its people are governed, the nation-state becomes a container of an imagined pure and homogenous society (Anderson, 1983) whose members represent recognised parts of the assumed whole.

Integration is simultaneously an imaginary of a desirable society and an objective of political governance according to which immigrants are expected to blend into the majority society and become invisible. Recent critiques target integration as a policy goal in the context of migration policies and as a focus of scholarly analysis (Meissner and Heil, 2020; Favell, 2019; Schinkel, 2018). Other contributions focus on how the normative principle translates into policies that target perceived minority groups (Korteweg, 2017; Penninx and Garcés-Mascareñas, 2016). Boundary markers like gender, class, race, religion and legal status strongly influence whom politics of integration affect and how (Anthias, 2014; Yuval-Davis, 2013). Integration policies not only perpetuate boundaries between perceived majorities and minorities, but also create distinctions between different minority groups, casting them as more or less compatible with the perceived majority.

In this article, I consider the ways in which integration is understood as resulting from how the term has been diffused through the media and public and political discourses. As such, the term addresses specific minorities and their often unsatisfactory ways of being and belonging in particular nation-states (see Rytter, 2019). So far, little attention has been paid to how the interplay of borders and boundaries inherent to fuzzy notions of integration affects individuals' everyday lives and meaning-making. The different ways in which members of perceived minority groups mobilise understandings of integration to adopt a certain position in society or to express their opinion relating to external ascriptions of (un)successful integration remain particularly underexplored (for an exception, see Bivand Erdal, 2013). For this reason, I examine how and why those targeted by public and political discourses around integration employ the concept themselves and turn it into a tool.

Theoretically, my analysis of how descendants of migrants experience, interpret, appropriate and modify understandings of integration in their everyday lives is inspired by de Certeau's reflections on the practice of everyday life (de Certeau, 1988). This theoretical anchorage helps me argue that, through the ways in which they employ understandings of integration, descendants of migrants 'find ways of using the constraining order of place or of the language. Without leaving the place where [they] have no choice but to live and which lays down its law for [them, they establish] within it a degree of plurality and creativity' (de Certeau, 1984: 30; italics in original). In this specific case, the constraining order of place manifests itself in understandings of integration that people apply to establish certain meanings or claim specific positions. By virtue of the fact that they are in between, descendants of migrants 'draw unexpected results from [their] situation' (de Certeau, 1984: 30).

According to de Certeau, it is through acts of enunciation that actors establish a present relative to time and place whilst being entangled in a network of places and relations (de Certeau, 1984: xiii). De Certeau refers to such everyday enunciations as 'tactics' (xix) through which the weak turn higher forces to their own ends. De Certeau seeks to establish how enunciations are constitutive of identity politics in a context that is structured by power relations. Although individuals may inhabit an inferior position in these power relations, they can subvert dominant laws, practices and representations from within. As a result, imposed knowledge, symbols and ideas – including integration – are manipulated by actors who have not produced them, but who are significantly affected by them (de Certeau, 1984: 32).

Although de Certeau's theorisation of everyday life practices grows out of studies of popular culture and consumption, it offers useful theoretical entry points for the issues at stake in this article. It is specifically the idea of enunciation, the articulation of words and meanings, that lends itself to analysing how persons employ understandings of integration. Understandings of integration thus serve as an entry point for the exploration of how the interplay of borders and boundaries affects individual meaning-making, perceptions of self and other and the ways in which people situate themselves in society. In the remainder of this article, I draw on qualitative interview data to demonstrate how descendants of migrants subvert dominant practices and representations from within.

Case study and methods

Empirically, this article draws on qualitative interview data that were generated as part of a research project examining how migrant descendants in Switzerland experience, interpret, appropriate and modify boundaries and experiences of discrimination in everyday life. The main focus of the overarching project was on encounters and engagements with institutional and everyday ethnicisation and otherness.

The research participants whose accounts inform this article were all born in Switzerland, and all except one have obtained Swiss citizenship. Yet, although research participants meet the formal criteria of belonging, they are often treated as if they were not fully part of Swiss society.

Between June 2016 and February 2018, the research team conducted 26 interviews with people whose parents came to Switzerland as immigrants from different countries of origin. All research participants are residents of the city of Zürich and aged between 25 and 40, and they come from different socio-economic, professional and religious backgrounds. Thematically, the interviews revolve around participants' life trajectories and experiences in Switzerland and focus specifically on experiences of othering and discrimination and the way participants attribute meaning to and act upon these experiences.

For the purpose of this article, the interviews were thematically coded according to explicit and implicit references to integration. The results were analysed according to the issues in relation to which research participants mobilise the term and how they position themselves vis-à-vis its meaning and implications. To this end, I applied a theoretical coding technique (Thornberg and Charmaz, 2014). Based on this systematic analysis, it is possible to identify different tactics revolving around enunciations of the concept of integration. In the remainder of this article, I present these tactical uses of integration and discuss how they reflect the interplay of borders and boundaries.

Mobilising understandings of integration

… to claim belonging or express non-belonging

In our interviews, participants often raised the issue of integration themselves, without prompting, in response to our questions. However, research participants mobilise understandings of integration in different ways, which is partly related to how they are situated in society and the interplay of borders and boundaries (Yuval-Davis, 2013). In line with their situatedness, they accept ascriptions of the perpetual immigrant other that have been imposed on them to varying extents. The account of Marta, a female participant of Albanian descent, for instance, reveals her ambiguous relationship with the concept of integration:

> As far as the Swiss context is concerned, I ask myself […]: 'Do we still need to discuss whether or not the second or third generation is integrated?' I get that we talk about integration in the case of refugees who have just arrived in Switzerland. But how can we talk about integration with regard to the third generation? How can we say, 'Yeah, integration means acquiring language skills'. Is that a joke? Our parents learned the language reasonably well, but there's no need to discuss the language skills of our generation. These are issues that I'm really eager to talk about publicly, and I find it important to express my own opinion. […] At some point it simply has to sink in. But that's hard.

While questioning the applicability of the concept of integration in relation to herself, Marta employs it to classify others, such as newly arrived refugees. Her tactic (de Certeau, 1988: xix) consists in drawing a boundary between her own position in Swiss society and the assumed position of newly arrived refugees. In this way, she claims belonging to Swiss society and refutes the otherness ascribed to her when the concept of integration is used in relation to migrant descendants. Hence, while she criticises the concept, she also mobilises it to measure the extent to which people form part of society. The boundaries that Marta perceives as separating her from Switzerland's majority society require the nation-state and its defining borders as a frame of reference.

Marta's example also demonstrates that perceptions of otherness based on national origin may extend over several generations. Her perceived position as the perpetually non-integrated other reflects the interplay of borders and boundaries in the sense that her parents' national origin supersedes the fact that she was born and socialised in Switzerland and is a Swiss citizen. Marta also turns her discontent about integration into a political project. She emphasises that she is eager to engage in critical discussions that promote a wider awareness of her perspective. Marta mobilises the concept of integration to claim belonging to Swiss society and put forward a socio-political agenda. It is necessary to underline, however, that participants speak from different social positions as far as markers such as race, class and gender are concerned, and that these differences influence how they use the concept of integration. Marta, for instance, identifies differences between the external ascriptions she confronts as a Swiss-born daughter of immigrant parents and those imposed on her partner, who originates from the same village as her parents but came to Switzerland only recently. The following example highlights such intersectional variations (Yuval-Davis, 2013) even more explicitly.

Peter, a young man of Cameroonian descent, uses the concept of integration when we speak about his experiences of everyday racism. He says that he has encountered racism more frequently in recent years, which he links to the increased number of migrants and asylum seekers from Eritrea:

> It's been worse since the Eritreans came. [...] I think this is important in my case. I was really well integrated. In fact, I was over-integrated. And then these Eritreans, Somalis and I don't know who came, and I just look too much like them. Now I have the feeling that everything's kaputt [that it has all been in vain]. That's how it is. [...] And I've been pretty pissed off since then. My status [in Swiss society] has literally dropped.

Peter's account underlines the generalising and racialising nature of integration, as a result of which individuals are reduced to members of certain constructed groups that are perceived as inferior, regardless of what they do or how they situate themselves. Peter confronts boundaries in the form of generalising and racist perceptions of himself as no different from other black men who are widely treated with considerable scepticism. He thought he had overcome these boundaries through his efforts at integration. He responds to these boundaries by distancing himself from the perceived others who – as he puts it – have damaged his status in Swiss society. Peter's tactic is similar to Marta's in the sense that the experience of boundaries prompts him to actively draw boundaries to claim belonging. However, being a male person of colour, the boundaries he confronts have different racist and gendered connotations. At the same time, Peter's example illustrates how borders impose their presence on social relations. He refers to distinct national groups whose arrival in Switzerland calls into question the position he believed he had achieved through successful integration. However, Peter's narrative also implies a critique of perceptions of Switzerland as a bounded community of white citizens.

Similarly to Peter, Simon, a research participant of Italian descent, employs the concept of integration when describing himself as part of Swiss society, which he frames in very positive terms. Integration to him means becoming Swiss and thus has a strong assimilationist connotation. However, due to his ethnic and migratory background Simon speaks from a very different position than Peter:

> I think that we Italians are well regarded here in Switzerland. We've successfully integrated and become part of society. That's why I think we're well respected. Well, obviously, if we exaggerate or are too noisy, it's normal that [it bothers people]. But that's come to bother me too, when an Italian makes too much noise. That's something typically Swiss that I've adopted.

Simon reproduces the idea that there is something genuinely Swiss that differs from what he considers as genuinely Italian. Without denying his Italian 'roots', he emphasises that his efforts to blend into Swiss society have been successful. To this end, he echoes a generalised perception of Italian migrants in Switzerland that differs strongly from the generalised perception Peter feels exposed to. Simon refers to his perception of annoying Italians as an indicator of his successful integration. For him there is a clear difference between being Swiss and being Italian. Hence, Simon reproduces widespread ideas of difference and sameness that are based on national origin but turns them to his own advantage. This is one way of making a dominant order function in another register (de Certeau, 1988).

The examples of Peter and Simon demonstrate that the ways in which people embrace the idea of integration are mediated by race and national origin. As a result of their ethnic backgrounds, their parents' migratory histories and the changing political and discursive environment in Switzerland, the boundaries that Peter and Simon confront and the boundaries they actively reproduce when using the concept of integration have very different, racialised connotations. The interplay between borders and boundaries thus manifests itself differently and has very different effects in these two cases. For this reason, their enunciations of integration result from specific positions in given power relations and different tactics. Simon demonstrates how borders in the form of certain nation-states and national backgrounds may acquire a positive connotation. Nationality-based boundary work still occurs, but – paradoxically – Simon mobilises nationality to make a case for belonging to Switzerland and Swiss society, a claim that Peter is far from able to make for himself. Both Peter and Simon employ the concept of integration to indicate their perceived position in Swiss society and the dominant representations that are constitutive of that position. However, Peter employs integration to specify his struggles and draw attention to the prevalence of racialised boundary work, whereas Simon uses it to tell a success story of belonging.

… to amend its meaning and scale of reference

Tim, whose parents originate from Bangladesh, deliberately inverts the logic of integration when he uses the concept to describe relationships among his peers when he was a teenager. In response to being asked about the ways in which distinctions between 'us' and 'them', and between majority and minority, marked his childhood and teenage friendships, he states:

> T: I think I wasn't very aware of it back then. And the Swiss kids [in our class at school] were so strongly integrated into us that we never noticed a big difference.

> C: In what sense were they 'integrated into you'?

T: Well, in the sense that… we had a certain atmosphere in that class and a particular way of engaging with and treating each other. It might have been different if the class had consisted entirely of Swiss kids; maybe it wouldn't have been like it was. It's probably a question of small nuances. That's why I say 'integrated into us'.

According to Tim's inverted logic, it is not the deficient immigrant minority that integrated into the dominant majority society, nor did the perceived majority adapt to the differences of the immigrant minority. Instead, integration is about establishing a form of joint communication and a way of getting along. However, Tim still reproduces boundaries along the lines of national belonging and membership in a nation-state by framing his social environment in terms of 'Swiss' and 'others'. Hence, although he makes a plea for integration in a more classical sense of the term (see for example Durkheim, 2006), his use of the concept is not devoid of borders and boundary work based on national origin.

Finally, Amanda, a participant of Serbian descent considers integration as subject to individual responsibility. Hence, she reproduces what Schinkel criticises as integration detached from societal responsibility and turned into a subject of individual responsibility (Schinkel, 2018):

Well, Switzerland is very open and tries to integrate everyone. I always think that if people don't manage [to integrate], it's their own fault. That's my opinion, obviously. Partly this comes from my own history. We wanted to be integrated, by all means, and we did it, although it wasn't easy. But now, when I look at the situation in the city of Zürich, I really think that whoever fails to integrate should blame themselves.

At first sight, Amanda fully embraces the principle of integration with its normative, neoliberal connotations, which place the burden on individuals' shoulders (Matejskova, 2013). In this way, she situates herself among those who have succeeded, whom she distinguishes from those who do not try hard enough. Again, we can discern a tactic of using the dominant understanding of integration to draw boundaries to one's own advantage. However, with her statement she also makes an important concession by underlining that it makes a significant difference which spatial and social entity one is trying to integrate into. Amanda refers to integration in the city of Zürich rather than Switzerland as a whole. Hence, it is not only parental descent and race that shape the position individuals are allocated and respond to when using the concept of integration; it also matters which social and spatial entity they refer to (Hadj Abdou, 2019). Whilst integration in Switzerland in general may be subject to a certain set of generalised expectations, integrating in a cosmopolitan place like the city of Zürich rest on very different requirements. Notwithstanding such variations, the normative underpinnings of integration as a principle prevail.

Other research participants echoed Amanda's spatial adjustments to the concept of integration. Several participants referred to the specificities of Zürich. For instance, Antonio, a young man of Spanish descent, emphasises that one can only be a part of Zürich by being different. People are not united through their shared ancestral origin, but through their lifestyle, worldview and attitudes. Through this emphasis, Antonio develops his own, highly locality-based definition of Swissness. Boundaries of belonging vary according to different localities and may be detached from the territorial and political entity of the nation-state and the borders that delineate it.

The interview sections above exemplify how participants engage with the boundaries that they experience themselves or which affect other groups in society. By applying different tactics, participants bend and sometimes undermine state-centred ideas of integration. To some extent, they challenge framings of membership in terms of national origin that necessarily involve the drawing of boundaries between those defined as the majority and minorities on the basis of various markers of difference. The tactics participants employ clearly reflect their ethnicised and racialised position in society as well as the social and spatial entity in relation to which they use the concept of integration.

Conclusion

With its focus on the interplay of borders and boundaries in understandings of integration, this article contributes to and establishes links between important areas of debate in contemporary migration studies. It adopts an original entry point to these debates by exploring how descendants of migrants mobilise understandings of integration to describe their experiences and sense of belonging or non-belonging to society.

The narratives featured in the empirical sections of this article demonstrate that migration and the crossing of national borders promote constant processes of self-definition and sometimes self-reinvention (van Houtum and van Naerssen, 2002) in the sense that people respond to ascriptions of being different from the imagined native Swiss majority society. The fact that our research participants did not migrate themselves but are mostly Swiss nationals who grew up in immigrant families accentuates the stickiness of perceived differences and related understandings of integration. Through enunciations of integration, they position themselves and others in light of certain normative principles that cannot be detached from the bounded entity of the nation-state. In other words, nation-state borders play an important role in shaping the boundaries our research participants confront and to which they respond with various tactics. One of these tactics, as my final examples demonstrate, consists in explicitly undermining such nation-state-centred principles of membership by referring to alternative scales of belonging, such as specific cities.

Otherness based on perceived non-belonging to the bounded national community forms an important dimension of our research participants' everyday lives in Switzerland. At the same time, however, confrontations with an integration paradigm may also lead to the reproduction of that very paradigm. Applying de Certeau's idea of tactics helps us understand the ways in which the people under study mobilise understandings of integration to substantiate their own perceived position in Swiss society or to allocate a certain position to other minority groups. Other identified tactics consist of moving away from and assigning different meanings to state-led understandings of integration, or relating integration to a different scale that is detached from the nation-state as a frame of reference for ideas of belonging.

My analysis of everyday understandings of integration demonstrates that the interplay between borders and boundaries not only informs specific fields of migration governance but also shapes individuals' sense of self and others and the ways in which people claim positions in society and pursue certain political objectives. Through tactics based on enunciations of integration, people establish a presence that is not only relative to time and place, but which also reflects the social position they are allocated as a result of ascribed markers of difference like race, class and gender that cause them to stick out as not fully integrated. In response to this – often inferior – position, enunciations of integration can be interpreted as micro-level identity politics through which people either subvert or assert dominant orders of belonging to Swiss society and their inherent interplay of borders and boundaries. A fuller understanding of the driving forces, effects and intersectional nature of these micro-level politics of belonging would require further research that goes beyond the Swiss context to unpack temporal and local parallels and contingencies.

References

Amelina, A. (2017). Transnationalizing inequalities in Europe : sociocultural boundaries, assemblages and regimes of intersection, Routledge research in transnationalism, First published 2017., New York, Routledge.

Anderson, B. (2019). 'New directions in migration studies: towards methodological de-nationalism', Comparative Migration Studies, vol. 7, no. 1, p. 36 [Online]. DOI: 10.1186/s40878-019-0140-8.

Anderson, B. R. (1983). Imagined communities: reflections on the origin and spread of nationalism, London, Verso.

Anthias, F. (2014) 'Beyond Integration: Intersectional Issues of Social Solidarity and Social Hierarchy', in Anthias, F. and Pajnik, M. (eds), Contesting Integration, Engendering Migration: Theory and Practice, Migration, Diasporas and Citizenship Series, London, Palgrave Macmillan UK, pp. 13–36 [Online]. DOI: 10.1057/9781137294005_2 (Accessed 14 August 2019).

Bakewell, O. (2008). 'Research Beyond the Categories: The Importance of Policy Irrelevant Research into Forced Migration', Journal of Refugee Studies, vol. 21, no. 4, pp. 432–453 [Online]. DOI: 10.1093/jrs/fen042.

Bauder, H. (2017). Migration, borders, freedom, Routledge studies in human geography, London, New York, Routledge, Taylor & Francis Group.

Bivand Erdal, M. B. (2013). 'Migrant Transnationalism and Multi-Layered Integration: Norwegian-Pakistani Migrants' Own Reflections', Journal of Ethnic and Migration Studies, vol. 39, no. 6, pp. 983–999 [Online]. DOI: 10.1080/1369183X.2013.765665.

Bukow, W.-D., Nikodem, C., Schulze, E. and Yildiz, E. (eds) (2007). Was heisst hier Parallelgesellschaft? Zum Umgang mit Differenzen, Interkulturelle Studien Leske Budrich, 1. Aufl., Wiesbaden, VS, Verl. für Sozialwiss.

Casas-Cortes, M., Cobarrubias, S., Genova, N. D., Garelli, G., Grappi, G., Heller, C., Hess, S., Kasparek, B., Mezzadra, S., Neilson, B., Peano, I., Pezzani, L., Pickles, J., Rahola, F., Riedner, L., Scheel, S. and Tazzioli, M. (2015). 'New Keywords: Migration and Borders', Cultural Studies, vol. 29, no. 1, pp. 55–87 [Online]. DOI: 10.1080/09502386.2014.891630.

de Certeau, M. (1988). The practice of everyday life, Berkeley, University of California Press.

Dahinden, J. (2016). 'A plea for the "de-migranticization" of research on migration and integration"', Ethnic and Racial Studies, vol. 39, no. 13, pp. 2207–2225 [Online]. DOI: 10.1080/01419870.2015.1124129.

Dahinden, J., Duemmler, K. and Moret, J. (2014). 'Disentangling Religious, Ethnic and Gendered Contents in Boundary Work: How Young Adults Create the Figure of "The Oppressed Muslim Woman"', Journal of Intercultural Studies, vol. 35, no. 4, pp. 329–348 [Online]. DOI: 10.1080/07256868.2014.913013.

Durkheim, E. (2006). On Suicide (trans. R. Buss), Sennett, R. (ed), Translation edition., London, Penguin Classics.

Fassin, D. (2005). 'Compassion and Repression: The Moral Economy of Immigration Policies in France', Cultural Anthropology, vol. 20, no. 3, pp. 362–387.

Fassin, D. (2011). 'Policing Borders, Producing Boundaries. The Governmentality of Immigration in Dark Times', Annual Review of Anthropology, vol. 40, no. 1, pp. 213–226 [Online]. DOI: 10.1146/annurev-anthro-081309-145847.

Fassin, D. (2020). Deepening divides : how territorial borders and social boundaries delineate our world, Anthropology, culture and society. Pluto Press, London.

Favell, A. (2019). 'Integration: twelve propositions after Schinkel', Comparative Migration Studies, vol. 7, no. 1, p. 21 [Online]. DOI: 10.1186/s40878-019-0125-7.

Grillo, R. D. (2003). 'Cultural Essentialism and Cultural Anxiety':, Anthropological Theory, vol. 3, no. 2 [Online]. DOI: 10.1177/1463499603003002002 (Accessed 11 February 2020).

Hadj Abdou, L. (2019). 'Immigrant integration: the governance of ethno-cultural differences', Comparative Migration Studies, vol. 7, no. 1, p. 15 [Online]. DOI: 10.1186/s40878-019-0124-8.

van Houtum, H. and van Naerssen, T. (2002). 'Bordering, Ordering and Othering', Tijdschrift voor Economische en Sociale Geografie, vol. 93, no. 2, pp. 125–136 [Online]. DOI: 10.1111/1467-9663.00189.

Kearney, M. (1991). 'Borders and Boundaries of State and Self at the End of Empire', Journal of Historical Sociology, vol. 4, no. 1, pp. 52–74 [Online]. DOI: 10.1111/j.1467-6443.1991.tb00116.x.

Korteweg, A. C. (2017). 'The failures of "immigrant integration": The gendered racialised production of non-belonging', Migration Studies, vol. 5, no. 3, pp. 428–444 [Online]. DOI: 10.1093/migration/mnx025.

Lamont, M. and Molnár, V. (2002). 'The study of boundaries in the social sciences', Annual Review of Sociology, vol. 28, pp. 167–195 [Online]. DOI: 10.1146/annurev.soc.28.110601.141107.

Matejskova, T. (2013). '"But One Needs to Work!": Neoliberal Citizenship, Work-Based Immigrant Integration, and Post-Socialist Subjectivities in Berlin-Marzahn', Antipode, vol. 45, no. 4, pp. 984–1004 [Online]. DOI: 10.1111/j.1467-8330.2012.01050.x.

Meissner, F. and Heil, T. (2020). 'Deromanticising integration: On the importance of convivial disintegration', Migration Studies, vol. Online first [Online]. DOI: 10.1093/migration/mnz056 (Accessed 20 February 2020).

Penninx, R. and Garcés-Mascareñas, B. (2016). 'The Concept of Integration as an Analytical Tool and as a Policy Concept', in Garcés-Mascareñas, B. and Penninx, R. (eds), Integration Processes and Policies in Europe: Contexts, Levels and Actors, IMISCOE Research Series, Cham, Springer International Publishing, pp. 11–29 [Online]. DOI: 10.1007/978-3-319-21674-4_2 (Accessed 17 May 2019).

Rytter, M. (2019). 'Writing Against Integration: Danish Imaginaries of Culture, Race and Belonging', Ethnos, vol. 84, no. 4, pp. 678–697 [Online]. DOI: 10.1080/00141844.2018.1458745.

Schinkel, W. (2018). 'Against "immigrant integration": for an end to neocolonial knowledge production', Comparative Migration Studies, vol. 6, no. 1, p. 31 [Online]. DOI: 10.1186/s40878-018-0095-1.

Taylor, C. (2004). Modern social imaginaries, Public planet books, Durham, Duke University Press.

Thornberg, R. and Charmaz, K. (2014). 'Grounded Theory and Theoretical Coding', in The SAGE Handbook of Qualitative Data Analysis, 55 City Road, SAGE Publications, Inc., pp. 153–169 [Online]. DOI: 10.4135/9781446282243 (Accessed 21 February 2020).

Wimmer, A. (2008). 'The making and unmaking of ethnic boundaries: A multilevel process theory', American Journal of Sociology, vol. 113, no. 4, pp. 970–1022 [Online]. DOI: 10.1086/522803.

Yuval-Davis, N. (2013). A Situated Intersectional Everyday Approach to the Study of Bordering, EU Borderscapes Working Papers.

July 2020
Volume: 17, **No**: 4, pp. 541 – 550
ISSN: 1741-8984
e-ISSN: 1741-8992
www.migrationletters.com

MIGRATION
LETTERS

First Submitted: 20 February 2019 Accepted: 16 January 2020
DOI: https://doi.org/10.33182/ml.v17i4.711

Feeling Strange. The Role of Emotion in Maintaining and Overcoming Borders and Boundaries

Paul Scheibelhofer[1]

Abstract

This article argues that a focus on emotion and affect helps to understand the processes of constructing and negotiating borders and boundaries critically. To do so, the article analyses two distinct yet connected cases in Austria: On the one hand, it discusses political discourse after the so-called "refugee crisis" of 2015 and shows, how a "politics of fear" was employed to regain control after a brief moment of relative freedom of movement. The second part of the analysis presents outcomes of an interview-based study with Austrians who engaged in a very intense form of refugee help by entering sponsorships with young male refugees. The analysis shows the role of emotions in legitimate restrictive border practices as well as their potential of creating solidarity across boundaries.

Keywords: *borders; boundaries; emotions; social processes; political discourse.*

Introduction

This article argues that a focus on emotion and affect helps to understand the processes of constructing and negotiating borders and boundaries critically. To do so, the article analyses two distinct yet connected cases in Austria: On the one hand, it discusses political discourse after the so-called "refugee crisis" of 2015 and shows, how a "politics of fear" (Wodak, 2015) was employed to regain control after a brief moment of relative freedom of movement. The second part of the analysis presents outcomes of an interview-based study with Austrians who engaged in a very intense form of refugee help by entering sponsorships with young male refugees. While, in the political sphere, negative emotions were used to gain public support for restrictive measures, the sponsorships are driven by emotions of pity, intimacy and solidarity in a context of complex power hierarchies. The analysis shows the role that emotions can play in maintaining boundaries and legitimating restrictive border politics. But it also shows how emotions can instigate the transgression of established boundaries of "us" and "them".

In this analysis, territorial borders, as well as social boundaries, are not viewed as static entities, but outcomes of complex social processes and practices. Following the seminal work of Fredrik Barth (1969) on ethnic groups and boundaries, social groups are seen as the outcome of "boundary work" rather than a sign of a pre-given cultural essence. Through "selective labelling" (Narayan, 2000) particular cultural practices are elevated to represent core aspects of a groups' authentic culture. The invention of traditions and linear historical narratives of cultural heritage facilitate the creation of imagined communities (Anderson, 1983) and the drawing of boundaries to others. As feminist and postcolonial theorists have shown, issues of race, gender and sexuality often intersect in these practices of constituting the self and the other (McClintock, 1995; Nagel, 2003). Rather

---
[1] Paul Scheibelhofer, Department of Educational Science, University of Innsbruck, Austria. E-mail: paul.scheibelhofer@uibk.ac.at

than asking how migration causes "integration problems" or "culture clashes", such a perspective asks, how social differences are produced in migration situations and how this is related to intersecting forms of power.

A sociological perspective also changes the view on borders. Rather than being seen as mere geographic demarcations, walls or fences, this perspective understands borders as complex outcomes of diverse practices, institutions, regulations and discourses (Newman, 2006). From this perspective, borders fulfil the function of shaping, channelling, decelerating and exploiting migration processes (Mezzadra & Neilson, 2013). In that, they are flexible and changing reactions to the flexible and changing practices of movement by migrants. Political migration discourses, as analysed in this article, can thus be seen as one facet of bordering practices (DeChaine, 2012). In these discourses, technologies and regulations of border control are made sense of, legitimised or challenged.

The analysis thus adopts a praxeological approach, interested in processes of *doing boundaries* and *doing borders*, while focusing on the role that emotions play in these processes. Such a focus on affect and emotions can shed light on some of the intricacies of the creation, reproduction and shifts in societal relations of difference. It also highlights some of the ways that the workings of boundaries and borders are entangled with each other. While boundaries and borders are distinct social institutions, they do not work detached from each other. Border regimes are codified practices of differentially allocating rights and resources to groups of people according to nationality and migration experiences. In that, they create an institutional context which naturalises the drawing of particular social boundaries and endows these practices of boundary making with social power. But border regimes, in turn, also need to be legitimised socially. A fact, which becomes particularly salient in times of crisis and political attempts to change established border regimes, as the below analysis shows. It documents, that drawing upon, and discursively shaping popular understandings of social boundaries between "us" and "them" is a political strategy to attain approval and legitimise particular migration policies. As the analysis also shows, emotions and affects are a key site where this entanglement between practices of doing border and doing boundary takes place. The first empirical case is an example of how emotions around questions of difference could successfully be shaped politically in order to push restrictive asylum laws. The second one, in turn, shows the power of emotions to instigate critique of and even opposition to established social boundaries and the border regime that codifies them. The relationship between emotions, boundaries and borders is thus complex and multifarious.

The personal is political: Theorising Emotions

The study of emotion and affect has recently proliferated in what has been termed "affective turn" or "emotional turn" in a range of academic disciplines (e.g. Clough & Halley, 2007; Greco & Stenner, 2008). Challenging the superiority of reason and objectivity over subjectivity and affect this research argues that emotions are not as private and personal as they often seem. Rather, emotions are understood as shaped by social context and relations of power. Through emotions, the personal is connected with the social, and it is through emotions, that the social is engaged with in everyday life.

Important predecessors to contemporary debates around emotion and affect were feminist scholars and activists (Gorton, 2007). Ever since the slogan "the personal is political" was coined, feminists engaged vigorously with the social nature of seemingly personal aspects of life (cf.

Cvetkovich, 2012: 133). They have long since identified the ideological and institutionalised division between a feminised private sphere (imagined to be a space of harmony and emotionality) vis-a-vis a masculinised public sphere (supposedly organised around rationality and reason) as a cornerstone to the reproduction of male dominance (Schneebaum, 2014). Engaging with the complexities of care work, feminists have highlighted how emotion is embedded in social relations of power both within private and corporate contexts (Hochchild, 1983) and the role that global hierarchies and colonial legacies can play therein (Gutiérrez Ródriguez, 2010).

Feminist literature thus "has long recognised the critical links between affect and gendered, sexualised, racalised and classed relations of power" (Pedwell & Whitehead, 2012: 116). As this literature argues, emotions are not detached from wider social structures of privilege and exploitation. *Who* can feel *what*, *where* and *when* is not a private matter but an expression of social relations and distinctions. In that, they are of central importance to the creation of groups and boundaries, as feminist theorist Sara Ahmed has pointed out. Drawing on the etymological origins of the term, Sara Ahmed (2004a) argues that emotions both "move" people as well as "connect" them with others. They have the potentiality, according to Ahmed, to "align" people towards others and thus form groups while moving them away from others. In her study, *The Cultural Politics of Emotions* Ahmed (2004b) shows the important role that the political sphere plays in shaping these processes of alignment and separation. As she shows, right-wing politics, in particular, manages to develop emotional thrust and persuasive power. This is accomplished by promoting the notion of a community of equals that "naturally" belongs to a particular territory. A territory its members are invited to *feel* to belong to and *feel* entitled to inhabit, undisturbed by strangers. In that, Ahmed diverges from approaches like "xenophobia", which locate the source of animosity to strangers in their objective difference. Rather, it is social processes that turn some strangers into "strange strangers" while at the same time drawing the contours of a community of insiders, to which its participants are emotionally attached. While socio-linguist Ruth Wodak importantly analysed the role of negative emotions in right-wing "politics of fear" (2015), Ahmed's approach highlights another aspect. Discussing the notion of "love" (for the nation, for the white family etc.) in right-wing discourses, Ahmed (2004b: 122) shows, that these discourses are never just directed *against* othered persons but also *for* selves and for what binds them together. Politics of fear and politics of love thus go hand in hand. What this theoretical literature shows is, that spurring particular emotions and thus establishing hegemonic "feeling rules" (Hochchild 1983) is an important facet of such politics, as emotions move people to identify with groups and boundaries and to get personally invested in their reproduction. A final body of work relevant to the present analysis is concerned with the contradictions of emotions in the context of helping.

While "regarding the pain of others" (Sonntag, 2003) and empathising with it can be a powerful motivator for solidarity and action, theorists have pointed to problematic aspects. Lauren Berlant criticised dynamics of "national sentimentality" (2000) when privileged citizens care for the suffering of marginalised people without engaging with the structural conditions that create differential life chances. The very act of compassionate help, Ildiko Zakarias points out, can enforce processes of boundary-making between helpers and the helped when "suffering and needs are emphasised on one side, while capacities and resources are stressed on the other" (Zakarias, 2015: 146). Focusing on the topic of the present article, we see that these problematic dynamics also exist in refugee contexts. As Castro Varela and Heinemann (2016) have shown in their analysis of refugee help projects in Europe after the so-called refugee crisis in 2015, "compassion" played an ambivalent role there. Depending on how it is employed, the authors argue, compassion can be both a powerful motivation to engage with the suffering of others in ways that empower refugees, or work as a justification for paternalistic interventions that mainly aim at demonstrating the magnificence of the helper. But problematic dynamics around emotion and affect not only take place on the level of individual refugee help projects. As Miriam Ticktin (2014) and Didier Fassin (2005) pointed out, refugee politics have recently shifted from a logic of rights to a "regime of humanitarianism" in which asylum seekers must demonstrate appropriate forms of (bodily) suffering in order to be seen as eligible for compassion and thus for legal protection. As also the Austrian case analysed below shows, this shift takes place within a wider political climate of increased mistrust against asylum seekers and the drafting of ever more restrictive policies (Fassin, 2011).

Negotiating borders and boundaries

In what follows, the role of emotion in the production and negotiation of borders and boundaries is analysed drawing on data from Austria. Two different, but connected, cases are analysed, namely anti-refugee politics after the so-called refugee crisis in 2015 and the practice of refugee sponsorship, where Austrian citizens care for and establish close ties with unaccompanied young male refugees. The analysis presents data from an ongoing study conducted by the author. For the analysis of political discourse, articles relating to refugee politics in Austrian news outlets (mainly *Die Presse* and *Der Standard*) that appeared from August 2015 to November 2016 were analysed using methods of Critical Discourse Analysis (Jäger, 2015). The analysis of refugee sponsorships is based on eleven qualitative interviews that took place between February and May 2017. Interviewees were Austrian citizens between the age of 40 and 65 that have engaged in sponsorships with young male refugees who came to the country in 2015, fleeing from Afghanistan, Syria and Iran. The interviews were analysed using the approach of Grounded Theory (Glaser & Strauss, 1967).

Anti-Refugee politics and fear of othered masculinities

Politics of emotion, Ahmed showed, often draw upon notions of gender, sexuality and race (Sara Ahmed, 2004b: 157). So too did politicians in Austria to regain control after the summer of 2015, when thousands of refugees crossed Austrian borders, leading to a partial break-down of the European border regime and creating a space of relative freedom of movement. The arrival of refugees was accompanied by a wave of public solidarity. Voluntary help projects ranged from first aid at camps or railway stations to practices such as providing legal advice or helping refugees to safely cross borders using private cars (Ataç, 2015). This public solidarity was sided by a political openness from the then ruling Parties *SPÖ* and *ÖVP*.[2] In August 2015 the *ÖVP*-Interior Minister demanded safe passage ways for refugees to Europe[3] and the *SPÖ*-Chancellor publicly criticised Hungary for its mistreatment of refugees.[4] In September, Austria decided to let thousands of refugees pass the borders and suspended border control, while the Austrian President lauded police and volunteers for their humanitarian engagement.[5] But this openness did not last long and soon after summer 2015, a gendered and racialised discourse of danger and threat arose within Austrian politics that fundamentally eventually changed public perceptions and later secured support for restrictive measures. Already in fall 2015, members of the right-wing *FPÖ* warned of the imminent

---

[2] As in several legislative periods before, the Christian-conservative *ÖVP* was in a coalition with the center-left *SPÖ* in 2015.
[3] In *Der Standard* of 28.08.2015.
[4] In *Die Presse* of *12.09.2015*.
[5] In *Die Presse* of 11.09.2015.

threat of an "Islamisation" of Austrian society by refugees and asked for a closing of the borders as the lax controls were "inviting terrorists into the country".[6] After that, the trope of the problematic male refugee was evoked repeatedly. As when the then-Interior Minister Sebastian Kurz (ÖVP) asked that "those who want to stay must respect our rules of coexistence. Amongst these basic values are the rule of law or gender equality"[7] or when the afore-mentioned Interior Minister called for barbed wire at Austria's Eastern borders because refugees "have become more impatient, more aggressive, more emotional over the last days and weeks".[8] While this drastic measure was not implemented due to resistance by the coalition-partner SPÖ, other ways of stopping refugees were found. A first measure was the introduction of an annual limit of asylum applications, which was introduced with the help of an "emergency decree" ('*Notverordnung*') and promoted by ministers of both ruling parties and the leader of the SPÖ[9] as a much needed corrective to save the small country of Austria from the "masses of refugees"[10] yet to come. But safeguarding Austrian borders was not enough. In January 2016, Minister Kurz stressed the need to close EU's external borders, even if this would "not work without ugly pictures".[11] In February he hosted a "West Balkans Conference" in Vienna, where the subsequent closing of the "Balkan route" was set in motion.

To regain political control after the crisis in 2015, refugee migration was reframed from an issue of humanitarianism and protection to a security threat. Central to the establishment of this "securitisation of migration" perspective (Bigo, 2002), was the depiction of male refugees as religio-culturally problematic and physically dangerous. The figure of the dangerous male refugee was important for this "politics of fear" (Wodak, 2015) to gain credibility and persuasive power. In that, a discourse of dangerous male refugees, that had been established in Austria in the 1990ies (Scheibelhofer, 2012) was taken up and merged with anti-Muslim sentiments. While this shift of perspective was well underway in winter 2015, the events during New Year's Eve 2016 in Cologne were used to further the new view on dangerous male refugees. At the beginning of 2016, German newspapers reported of "North African-looking" men attacking German women on a public square during New Year's Eve festivities. While concrete information was scarce, newspapers soon invoked gendered racist imageries (Boulila/Carri, 2017) in reports about attacks of up to 1.000 young male refugees in Cologne and other cities.

Austrian politicians soon took up this discourse and identified a misogynistic Arab culture and archaic Muslim religiosity of male refugees as the cause of the incident. Thus FPÖ politicians warned of Muslim refugees undermining hard-won women's rights,[12] Minister Kurz stated that he already had "anticipated tensions, assaults and violent clashes"[13] and a politician of the right-leaning *Team Stronach* explained that this was to be expected when thousands of young Muslim men without wives came to Europe.[14] Many of these statements blamed lax refugee policies as well as the naïve "goodwill" of parts of the society for making the attacks possible. Consequences were thus called for, and the demands ranged from completely closing the borders to stricter deportation

---

[6] In Die Presse of 25.09.2015, all direct quotes have been translated into English by the author.

[7] In *Die Krone* of 22.09.2015.

[8] On the national radio station *Ö1* on 28.10.2015.

[9] In *Kleine Zeitung* of 21.02.2015.

[10] From an article published on the website of the ÖVP, www.oevp.at/team/kurz/Kurz-Wir-muessen-Obergrenzen-festlegen.psp, accessed on 14.11.2016.

[11] In *Die Welt* of 13.01.2016.

[12] Press release of the *FPÖ* from 07.01.2016.

[13] In *Die Welt* of 13.01.2016.

[14] Press release of the *Team Stronach* of 07.01.2016.

laws and compulsory DNA-testing of all male refugees at EU borders to curfews for male refugees. To counter the perceived threat, several cities founded vigilante groups.[15]

The debates after the incidents in Cologne added sexualised imageries to the already unfolding politics of fear against male refugees. These "ethnosexual" (Nagel, 2003) imageries combined notions of racial difference with dangerous sexuality, building on long established colonialist ideas of a pervert, archaic Orient, as already critically discussed by Edward Said (1979). Taking up these long established imageries, the gendered and racialised discourse alluded to fears and called for action. It positioned white women as in danger of being violated by sexually devious refugee men and accorded white men the role as saviours of these women. It made use of a discursive strategy that Ahmed (2000: 29) termed "stranger danger", by which some-bodies are identified as dangerous bodies and thus fixing them as "strange strangers" against whom protective measures need to be taken. Stranger danger creates "suspects", with seemingly perilous bodies and mores, and "subjects" who are united in vigilance and fear of the danger emanating from strangers. But the imperilled women in this narrative symbolically stood in for more than just themselves, as politicians drew upon what Sara Farris (2017) termed a "femonationalist" discourse, in which supposedly stark differences in gender relations between societies of the West vs the global rest are invoked in order to draw boundaries between an enlightened "us" and problematic strangers. The need to protect white women from sexual harm was thus linked to the need to protect the nation from male refugees in general. In Austria, the process of reframing refugee migration as dangerous was successful: In early elections in 2017, both the ÖVP and the FPÖ won seats and formed a new right-wing government with a strong anti-refugee agenda. Refugee-help projects were increasingly viewed with suspicion and cut back considerably. The new government hence introduced several restrictions in migration and refugee law without sparking major public criticism, on the contrary, enjoying high approval rates.

Shifting the dominant feeling rules towards refugees was obviously successful. The universalistic notion of refugees as being individuals in need of help and aid was shifted after the "crisis" of 2015. Employing a gendered and racialised politics of fear, stark boundaries between dangerous others and an imperilled self were drawn. This formed a fertile ground to gain approval for new restrictions in the Austrian migration regime.

Negotiating hegemonic feeling rules in refugee sponsorships

What happens, when the social boundaries promoted by a politics of fear are subverted and divisions between "us" and "them" are transgressed? As the following analysis of refugee sponsorships with young unaccompanied male refugees shows, such transgressions can be a site of friction and contradictions but also a powerful driver of social change. Emotion and affect, the analysis also shows, play a central role in these dynamics.

In creating intimate and family-like relationships with those deemed dangerous strangers, the women and men who engaged in these sponsorships obviously subverted the "feeling rules" (Hochchild, 1983) promoted by politics of fear. But building this closeness across boundaries did not happen straight forward. None of the interviewed sponsors initially planned to enter in a refugee-sponsorship in the first place. Rather, becoming a sponsor was the outcome of a process that began with coincidental encounters during acts of spontaneous help during summer 2015 and gradually intensified. As one sponsor described it: "It was a matter of feeling, you know? I never actually had

---

[15] On the national radio station Ö1 on 11.02.2016.

the plan to get a godson." For several interviewees feelings played a complex role in this process: While compassion motivated them to engage in refugee help in the first place, it was sympathy that drew them closer to the individual young men that they would later establish sponsorships with. This sympathy was often stimulated by character traits described by the sponsors as "cleverness", "intelligence" or "ambition". The young men needed to show willingness to learn German, go to school or take up work. For the relationship between helper and refugee to intensify beyond the point of mere assistance, the young men thus had to distinguish themselves by a likeable and promising personality.

At the time of the interviews, the sponsorship-arrangements differed to some degree. However, strong ties had established in all cases and nearly all sponsors either explicitly stated that they saw the young men as "part of the family" or at least drew strong parallels to familial ties when describing their relationships. To reach this closeness all parties involved – the refugees, the helpers and also their close kin – had to transgress boundaries and open up to persons that were strangers not long ago. This process could involve frictions and hesitations from all sides. Thus, one sponsor recounted that she disliked being called "mum" by the young man at first, "because it just did not feel like it for me". Eventually, most sponsorships took on family-like forms and ended up feeling much like a new child entered the families. This, in turn, caused trouble in some cases. The new person in the family caused jealousy amongst children, parents as well as partners of sponsors, which could be resolved in several cases but lead to one cancellation of a sponsorship as well as one break up of a partnership. Some sponsors thus had to deal with struggles over the distribution of attention, affect and care work within their family. But also the young refugees themselves had to overcome boundaries and sponsors recounted that some of the men were very timid and introverted at the beginning of the relationship, while others seemed to distrust the sponsors' motivations at first. Most of the young men also stayed in contact with their actual parents and kin in countries across the globe. For them, entering into the sponsorship meant having to juggle relationships and loyalties within a complex, extended, transnational family. The sponsorships were thus sites of "doing family" (Hertz, 2006) under complicated and a-typical conditions. But framing the relationship as "almost family" allowed the persons involved to transgress boundaries and establish very strong and intimate ties with recent strangers. Here, it was the *female* sponsors in particular, that tended to establish closer relationships to the young men due to the gendered division of labour amongst sponsors. While the husbands engaged more in helping solve practical and legal problems, the female sponsors spent more time actually communicating with them. Listening to the young men's thoughts, experiences, stories and grievances created a bond between the godsons and their "sponsor-moms" that did not exist in a similar way with the "dads". Several of the women interviewed told about the intense closeness that had established between them and the young men.

However intimate the sponsorships became, they were not free from hierarchies and power differences. Thus sponsors recounted instances of frustration, when the young men did not react appropriately to offers by the sponsors, e.g. by not attending a German course organised and paid for by the sponsor or not accepting the old clothes that sponsors and their friends collected. In one case, the sponsor explicitly told the young refugee that he could only go on staying in their home when he visited the school and finished with a degree, as she did not want to watch him become a "problem case". In these situations, the power differences in relations of help and assistance surfaced. While the sponsors felt pride about their altruism, these situations pushed the refugees in recurring situations of having to accept, to abide and be thankful. As Kerstin Duemmler (2014) argued, this "paradigm of thankfulness" is a recurring feature in contexts of ethnic boundary making. Analysing social relations in Swiss schools, Duemmler shows how migrant youth was relegated to the position of "guests" and were thus expected to "adapt to local customs and show gratitude for the hospitality of their patrons" (Duemmler 2014: 192, translation P.S.) for being allowed to live in Switzerland. As the case of refugee sponsorships indicates, this need for thankfulness does not arise in a social vacuum but is connected to existing negative stereotypes. Showing gratitude and thankfulness was one of the many acts expected from the young refugees, to prove that they were not one of the problematic foreign men. Never the less, in some sponsorships, issues of gender norms and the supposed backwardness of the young men became recurring issues of debate, that one sponsor commented on in the interview with the half-joking words: "After all, he is a Muslim macho."

These struggles notwithstanding, all interviewed sponsors formulated a clear and decisive critique of the dominant representations of young male refugees on the basis of their experiences. This critique was not only articulated against representations in media and political discourse but also entered the personal arena. Virtually all sponsors had experienced disagreements, fights and alienation amongst friends and family. Sponsors told about heated discussions at parties or Christmas dinners and about relatives that did not approve of the sponsors bringing along their godson to vacations. Through the young men's stories, sponsors also learned about the realities of discrimination and racism in Austrian society. The extend of which shocked several of the interviewees, be it negative experiences with schools or in trying to find a job, at legal hearings or with racial profiling of the police in public space.

Facing these experiences amongst relatives and in wider society, a spill-over effect of the strong emotional connection they had established with the young refugees became visible. They confronted friends and families as well as authorities and institutions such as the police. Several sponsors eventually began to participate in political groups for refugee rights and became regular attendees of demonstrations against deportations, refugee laws and the government in general. Also, the relationship with the young men had pushed them further and further as to what they were ready to invest in order to help them start a successful life in Austria or to prevent deportation, "hiding him if needed" as sponsors stated, using almost identical words. Reflecting upon their own development during the sponsorship, several interviewees were astonished about their decisiveness and courage. But, in the words of one interviewee, refugee sponsorships have the tendency to "radicalise you".

Conclusion

This article argues, that acts of "doing border" should not be understood as happening detached from processes of "doing boundary". Focussing on the role of emotions was proposed as a way to grasp these intricate entanglements better. One context, where this was shown, was the political efforts to regain control after the Austrian migration regime was virtually put out of order by refugees in summer 2015.

In such moments of crisis and reconfiguration of social structures oftentimes, their workings become more apparent. As the analysis showed, new and stricter migration laws directed against refugees could not be introduced right away, against the then existing wave of solidarity for the men, women and children arriving in great numbers in dire need for help. The so-called "welcome culture" of this period can thus be understood as a phase, where considerable fractions of society put into question the drawing of social boundaries along ethnocentric and nationalist lines. These lines had to be redrawn, in order to legitimate the political introduction of restrictive migration laws and gain public support for these measures. The analysis claims that emotions and affect were a central site where this shift was accomplished. After the summer of 2015, a political discourse in Austria gradually proliferated, that shifted the perspective on refugees as a humanitarian issue to a symptom of crisis and danger. A gendered and sexualised politics of fear, circling around imageries of dangerous foreign masculinity, managed to establish new "feeling rules" and the re-drawing of boundaries in the name of saving women and saving society as a whole.

These politics of emotion were widely successful in reframing the refugee question but did not go uncontested. In establishing particularly intimate relationships with unaccompanied male refugees, sponsorships are a site, where boundaries are transgressed. This transgression is not devoid of frictions and, as the analysis showed, not completely free of the powerful dynamics of boundary making. Hierarchies, imageries, expectations, and dependencies structure this relationship and hinder an encounter as equals.

But the analysis also showed, how the intimacy and emotional attachments that developed in many of these sponsorships can unsettle established not only social boundaries between "us" and "them" but also spur critique against a restrictive "doing borders" on a societal level. The intimacy and emotional connection created in these sponsorships had the potential to turn into solidarity with those deemed dangerously different. It would thus be wrong to blind out issues of emotions as "merely personal" from the analysis of boundary and bordering practices. The analysis documents that emotions can have divergent effects and lead both to "social reproduction and social change" (Gould, 2010: 32). And it shows that suffering of intimate others can lead to anger as a political emotion (Lorde, 1984), motivating engagement with how borders and boundaries are drawn and transgressing spheres of the personal and the political.

References

Ahmed, S. (2000). Strange encounters: Embodied Others in Post-Coloniality. London: Routledge.
Ahmed, S. (2004a). "Collective Feelings: Or, the Impressions Left by Others". Theory, Culture and Society, 21 (2): 25-42. DOI: 10.1177/0263276404042133
Ahmed, S. (2004b). The cultural politics of emotion. Edinburgh: Edinburgh University Press.
Anderson, B. (1983). Imagined communities: Reflections on the origin and spread of nationalism. London: Verso.
Ataç, I. (2015). "Freiwilligenarbeit als Notnagel oder Neuformulierung der Zivilgesellschaft?". Kurswechsel, 4/2015: 80-85.
Barth, F. (1969). Ethnic groups and boundaries. The social organisation of culture difference. Boston: Little, Brown.
Berlant, L. (2000). "The subject of true feeling: Pain, privacy and politics". In: S. Ahmed, J. Kilby, C. Lury, M. McNeill and B. Skeggs (eds.) Transformations. Thinking Through Feminism. London: Routledge, pp. 33-47.
Bigo, D. (2002). "Security and Immigration: Toward a Critique of the Gouvernmentality of Unease". Alternatives: Global, Local, Political, 27: 63-92. DOI: 10.1177/03043754020270S105
Boulila, S. C. and Carri, C. (2017). "On Cologne: Gender, migration and unacknowledged racisms in Germany". European Journal of Women's Studies, 24 (3): 286–293. DOI: 10.1177/1350506817712447
Castro Varela, M. d. M. and Heinemann, A. (2016). "Mitleid, Paternalismus, Solidarität. Zur Rolle von Affekten in der politisch-kulturellen Arbeit". In: M. Ziese and C. Gritschke (eds.) Geflüchtete und Kulturelle Bildung. Formate und Konzepte für ein neues Praxisfeld. Bielefeld: transcript, pp. 51–66.
Clough, P. T. and Halley, J. (eds.) (2007). The Affective Turn: Theorising the Social. Durham: Duke University Press.
Cvetkovich, A. (2012). "Depression Is Ordinary: Public Feelings and Saidiya Hartmann's Lose your Mother". Feminist Theory, 13 (2): 131-146. DOI: 10.1177%2F1464700112442641
DeChaine, D. R. (2012). Border rhetorics. Citizenship and identity on the US-Mexico frontier. Tuscaloosa: University of Alabama Press.
Duemmler, K. (2014). Symbolische Grenzen. Zur Reproduktion sozialer Ungleichheit durch ethnische und religiöse Zuschreibungen. Bielefeld: transcript.

Farris, S. (2017). In the Name of Women's Rights. The Rise of Femonationalism. Durham: Duke University Press.

Fassin, D. (2005). "Compassion and Repression: The Moral Economy of Immigration Policies in France". Cultural Anthropology, 20 (3): 362–387. DOI: 10.1525/can.2005.20.3.362

Fassin, D. (2011). "Policing Borders, Producing Boundaries. The Governmentality of Immigration in Dark Times". Annual Review of Anthropology, 40: 213-226. http://www.annualreviews.org/doi/full/10.1146/annurev-an40

Glaser, B. and Strauss, A. (1967). The Discovery of Grounded Theory. London: Weidenfeld & Nicolson.

Gorton, K. (2007). "Theorising Emotion and Affect: Feminist Engagements". Feminist Theory, 8 (3): 333-348. DOI: 10.1177%2F1464700107082369

Gould, D. (2010). "On Affect and Protest". In: J. Staiger, A. Cvetkovich and A. Reynolds (eds.) Political Emotions. New Agendas in Communication. New York: Routledge, pp. 18-44.

Greco, M. and Stenner, P. (eds.) (2008). Emotions: A Social Science Reader. London: Routledge.

Gutiérrez Ródriguez, E. (2010). Migration, Domestic Work and Affect: A Decolonial Approach on Value and the Feminization of Labor. New York: Routledge.

Hertz, R. (2006). "Talking about 'Doing Family'". Journal of Marriage and Family, 68 (4): 796-799. DOI: 10.1111/j.1741-3737.2006.00293.x

Hochchild, A. (1983). The managed heart. Commercialisation of human feeling. Berkeley: University of California Press.

Jäger, S. (2015). Kritische Diskursanalyse. Münster: Unrast Verlag.

Lorde, A. (1984). "The Uses of Anger: Women Responding to Racism". In: A. Lorde (ed.) Sister Outsider. Berkeley: Crossing Press, pp. 124-133.

McClintock, A. (1995). Imperial Leather: Race, Gender, and Sexuality in the Colonial Contest. New York: Routledge.

Mezzadra, S. and Neilson, B. (2013). Border as Method, or, the Multiplication of Labor. Durham: Duke University Press.

Nagel, J. (2003). Race, Ethnicity and Sexuality: Intimate Intersections, Forbidden Frontiers. Oxford: Oxford University Press.

Narayan, U. (2000). "Undoing the 'Package Picture' of Cultures". Signs: Journal of Women in Culture and Society, 25 (4): 1083-1086. DOI: 10.1086/495524

Newman, D. (2006). "On borders and power: A theoretical framework". Journal of Borderlands Studies, 18 (1): 13-25. https://doi.org/10.1080/08865655.2003.9695598

Pedwell, C. and Whitehead, A. (2012). "Affecting Feminism: Questions of Feeling in Feminist Theory". Feminist Theory, 13 (2): 115-129. DOI: 10.1177%2F1464700112442635

Said, E. W. (1979). Orientalism. New York: Vintage Books.

Scheibelhofer, P. (2012). "From Health Check to Muslim Test: The Shifting Politics of Governing Migrant Masculinity". Journal of Intercultural Studies, 33 (3): 319-332. DOI: 10.1080/07256868.2012.673474

Schneebaum, A. (2014). "All in the family: patriarchy, capitalism, and love". In: A. Jónasdóttir and A. Ferguson (eds.) Love: a question for the twenty-first century. New York: Routledge, pp. 127–140.

Sonntag, S. (2003). Regarding the Pain of Others. London: Penguin Books.

Ticktin, M. (2014). "Transnational Humanitarianism". Annual Review of Anthropology, 43: 273-289. https://www.annualreviews.org/doi/10.1146/annurev-anthro-102313-030403

Wodak, R. (2015). The politics of fear. What right-wing populist discourses mean. London: SAGE.

Zakarias, I. (2015). "The Production of Solidarity: A Case Study of Voluntary School Programs of Hungarian Ethnic Kin Support". In: J. Kleres and Y. Albrecht (eds.) Die Ambivalenz der Gefühle: Über die verbindende und widersprüchliche Sozialität von Emotionen. Wiesbaden: Springer, pp. 145-169.

July 2020
Volume: 17, **No**: 4, pp. 551 – 558
ISSN: 1741-8984
e-ISSN: 1741-8992
www.migrationletters.com

MIGRATION
LETTERS

First Submitted: 22 August 2019 Accepted: 6 May 2020
DOI: https://doi.org/10.33182/ml.v17i4.839

Everyday Re-Bordering and the Intersections of Borderwork, Boundary Work and Emotion Work amongst Romanians Living in the UK

Kathryn Cassidy[1]

Abstract

This article explores the intersections of borderwork and boundary work in everyday encounters in the UK. It focuses on the experiences of Romanian nationals, who between 2007 and 2014 were subject to transitional controls, which are understood as a form of everyday re-bordering of the de-bordered space of the EU that denied equal access to the labour market and state support. These controls were accompanied by a range of bordering discourses in the media and political circles that firmly situated Romanians outside of the UK's contemporary political project of belonging. This article argues that in order to understand borderwork in everyday life, we need to explore how it relates to boundary work, i.e. the differential positionalities of Romanians within social hierarchies, as well as their experiences of and engagement with emotion work. The data analysed comes from participant observation with Romanian communities in London and the North East of England in the period from 2009 to 2014.

Keywords: *Bordering, boundaries; emotion work; European migration; transitional controls.*

Introduction

In this article, I argue that the everyday discourses used to exclude Romanian nationals in the UK in the period from 2007 to 2014 should be understood as emerging at the juncture of borderwork and boundary work. Recent scholarship in border studies has focused upon the increasing internal reach of bordering practices and processes (Balibar, 2004; Yuval-Davis et al. 2018, 2019) and the growing involvement of residents in formal borderwork, i.e. checking the immigration status of others to determine their access to a range of services (Yuval-Davis et al., 2018; Cassidy, 2018). However, the efficacy of the internalisation of state borderwork is heightened by b/ordering and othering (van Houtum and van Naersson, 2002) processes and practices, which normalise not only everyday bordering (Yuval-Davis et al., 2018) itself but also the orders underpinning it. These b/orders seek to create hierarchies of belonging, which are co-constituted with socio-cultural boundaries, i.e. they intersect with class, race, gender, sexuality (Yuval-Davis, 2013).

Whilst firewall bordering, i.e. the filtering of would-be border-crossers through formal immigration (or bordering) regimes (Walters, 2006; Yuval-Davis et al., 2019), may permit movement across borders for certain groups, socio-cultural boundaries can continue to prevent such border crossings long after formal barriers are removed. In addition, even when international borders have been crossed, residents (new and old) find themselves b/ordered in everyday life by such hierarchies that would cast them as 'out of place' or less 'in place' than others. In this article, I focus on the period of transitional controls, when Romanians had the right to move to and take up

---

[1] Kathryn Cassidy, Department of Geography and Environmental Sciences, Northumbria University, Newcastle upon Tyne, United Kingdom. E-mail: kathryn.cassidy@northumbria.ac.uk.

Copyright @ 2020 MIGRATION LETTERS
Transnational Press London

residence in the UK but had restricted permission to work and limited access to social security. I explore the ways in which Romanian citizens living in the UK at that time were not only subject to border-and-boundary work but also actively *contested* this work in everyday encounters. I argue that engagement in these dialogical practices of contestation is shaped by self-management of emotions or 'emotion work' (Hochschild, 1983). By focusing on the agency of minoritised groups to contest b/ordering discourses, I seek to re-consider analysis (Verhage, 2014), which suggests that border-and-boundary work sediments over time and is carried unconsciously by members of minoritised groups.

I begin with a summary of theoretical work that considers the interplay of borderwork and boundary work before moving to the question of emotion work, emotional bordering and emotional borderwork. This conceptual framing is then followed by a short methodology and brief description of the transitional controls for Romanian and Bulgarian nationals, which were in place in the UK from 2007 to 2014. The final section of the article presents the analysis of empirical data drawn from ethnographic fieldwork with Romanian communities in London and the North East of England.

Borderwork and boundary work

[I]n any consideration of borders and power relations we need to ask further questions, such as who is doing the enclosing and who is in a position to create a border? In short, who performs the borderwork? (Rumford, 2008: 2). Rumford (2008) highlights that borderwork is very much undertaken by 'ordinary citizens' and argues that this means that 'the border' is something over which the same 'ordinary citizens' have control. However, recent changes in immigration legislation in the UK, mean that *formal* or *state* borderwork is now required of many more residents as a result of the increasing internal reach of bordering processes and practices, or *everyday bordering* (Yuval-Davis et al., 2018). As other residents undertake checks on the immigration status of others in a range of everyday encounters – opening a bank account, registering with a doctor, renting a property, getting a job – they undertake the work of bordering the state. The incorporation of more and more people into state borderwork is far more extensive than the voluntary reporting on others undertaken by 'citizen-detectives' (Vaughan-Williams, 2008). The embedding of state bordering practices more deeply into everyday life has been accompanied by increased sanctions – civil and criminal – for those who do not comply (Yuval-Davis et al., 2019; Cassidy, forthcoming). Therefore, whilst more and more residents may be undertaking borderwork, if that borderwork is mandated and potentially punishable by the state, we need to consider the very real constraints and how much 'control' we can really consider residents to have over this.

Yet, Rumford does not limit borderwork to that undertaken formally on behalf of the state: *The importance of borderwork is that it causes us to rethink the issue of who is responsible for making, dismantling and shifting borders, rather than rely upon the assumption that this is always the business of the state.* (Rumford, 2013: 170)

Borderwork is part of a wider set of processes and practices through which the state becomes normalised in everyday life (Navaro-Yashin, 2002). Reeves (2014: 6) defines borderwork as 'the messy, contested, and often intensely social business of making territory "integral"'. Her focus is on an emergent international border, but she highlights that 'the work of state spatiality is not confined to the physical edges of the cartographic limits, or those wearing the border guard's uniform' (ibid: 245). Therefore, we cannot see borderwork *within* the UK as being restricted to those co-opted into undertaking immigration checks in everyday life on behalf of the state over which they have limited control. State bordering is embedded in internal social processes and practices of ordering and wider discourses of 'othering' (van Houtum et al., 2005; van Houtum and van Naersson, 2002). Such hierarchies may appear to be stable at times but are often contested and dynamic. Boundary work is undertaken by individuals and institutions in order to situate themselves and in relation to others according to categories, such as gender, class and race (Bartkowski & Read, 2003; Anthias and Yuval-Davis, 2005) and involves processes and practices of differentiation, inclusion and exclusion. Examples of this interplay of borderwork and boundary work that frequently emerge in the UK media include the questioning of the 'genuineness' of young male asylum seekers (Griffiths, 2017) and the use of racialised and impoverished images of Romanian Roma to place Romania outside of the EU as a political project of belonging (Wemyss and Cassidy, 2017).

Emotional Borderwork and Emotion Work

Potter and Meier (2020) have developed the concept of *emotional borderwork* to explore the emotional labour (Hochschild, 1983) of undertaking the state borderwork described above for professionals within the UK's national health service. In Hochschild's original thesis, a distinction is made between the self-management of 'emotion work' and the more public display of emotional labour, often within organisations and workplace settings. It is this self-management of emotions or emotion work within some settings with which I am concerned here. In particular, the ways in which some Romanian nationals, but not others, performed emotion work 'unconsciously in personal relationships in everyday life' (Kawale, 2004: 567).

Our reactions to others are not individual but shaped by our socio-cultural context. *[I]n our social interactions with other people, we observe conventions, and we obey the demand for a particular rhythm of encounter. In this manner, we are caught in an intersubjective dance that smoothly takes place within a certain socio-cultural milieu* (Verhage, 2014: 98).

Verhage (2014) argues that dominant groups and their assumptions about minoritised populations can 'occupy' the bodies of the minoritised, so that they carry these b/orders around with them. Through these 'occupations', socio-cultural boundaries sediment; that is to say they become habitual over time and shape a dominant flow. They mean that our encounters with others are often pre-determined, unconscious and reinforce these flows rather than challenge them. Yet, Verhage's description seems to marginalise the agency of minoritised groups to shape these boundaries in their emergence. Whilst dominant groups may seek to 'embrace' different bodies unequally, not all minoritised bodies are equally positioned. Yuval-Davis (2015) argues that it is important to explore not only social positioning in relation to axes of oppression but also to consider the specific context; helping us to understand how those who may similarly be positioned socially develop differing situated gazes in a specific time-place. Some bodies are better-positioned to exert control in relation to borderwork in certain circumstances than others. Whilst certain categorisations, e.g. race, gender, can be viewed as systematic asymmetry (Verhage, 2014, 99), others are better understood as momentary, fleeting, specific to the time-place.

Methodology

This article is based primarily upon participant observation with Romanians living in South London from April 2009 to April 2014[2]. The research developed through contact with a number of Romanians from a village in Suceava county in Romania, where I had undertaken participant observation from June 2008 to January 2009. When I returned to the UK, some people from the village had already moved to South London for work and got in touch with me, often to ask for help and support with employment, taxes and schooling. From April 2009, when I was based in London, I was frequently invited to and attended social occasions at the homes of these families at weekends. Informed consent was obtained verbally from all participants following a thorough explanation of the research. The findings presented here have also been discussed with some of the participants and refined based upon feedback and clarifications received. Participant observation enabled not only informal, unstructured interviewing, but also the observation of non-verbal communication and embodied, affective responses to both interactions with myself as the researcher and with other people present. All these data were recorded every day in fieldwork notes and were essential to understanding the emotionality of the field.

Everyday Re-Bordering and Romanian Citizens in the UK

The de-bordering of the UK for Romanian nationals that came with EU membership in 2007 was accompanied by an intensification of everyday re-bordering, which sought to 'border' the UK from within by preventing equal access to employment and state welfare benefits through what were known as the 'transitional controls'. The controls resulted from political campaigns and media discourses against EU migration to the following the Union's 2004 enlargement (Yuval-Davis et al., 2018). Until 2014, Romanian nationals had to gain worker authorisation for employment and after 12 months of paid employment were discharged from the scheme and gained the 'right to reside', which enabled them to access state welfare benefits. The need to gain authorisation in order to be employed was an important part of the uncertainty that framed life and its emotionality for Romanian migrants in the UK during this period.

Following the removal of the transitional controls in 2014, the UK government continued to border the welfare state by giving citizens of other EU member states looking for work access to Universal Credit[3] for just three months. Failure to find work in this period would lead to a denial of the 'right to reside' and, consequently, of access to state support.

In addition to a state bordering once they are in the UK, Romanian citizens, in particular, were also the focus of intensive b/ordering discourses in the media prior to the removal of the transitional controls in January 2014 (Wemyss and Cassidy 2017). Coverage in the press used words such as 'swamp', 'flood' and 'flock' to describe the removal of the controls and the potential for higher levels of migration from Romania and Bulgaria to the UK (ibid). Reports in the media also drew upon images of poverty in both countries, particularly amongst Roma communities, in order to support their narratives, as well as making specific reference to the labour market as 'overstretched' and nationalising labour market opportunities through terms such as 'UK jobs' (ibid). As we shall see in the final section of illustrative examples below, these discourses entered into everyday

---

[2] Some further participant observation took place with Romanians living in the North East of England from 2014 based primarily on connections to those I had met during the initial phase of fieldwork in London, as well as on return visits to London whilst I continued to work on a London-based research project until the end of 2016.

[3] Universal Credit is the support offered by the UK government to those with low incomes or who are out of work.

encounters, where we can explore the intersections of borderwork, boundary work and emotion work.

Borderwork, boundary work and emotion work in everyday life

Nelu was a man in his thirties from a village in Suceava county, who moved to London in 2007 and by the end of 2014 was working on a temporary basis in a logistics' warehouse in the North East of England. He, and other Romanian nationals, often described difficulties in developing relationships with colleagues, who were from white British backgrounds. It emerged that some of these difficulties were the result of what they felt to be misconceptions about them, which were based upon dominant public discourses (Wemyss and Cassidy, 2017). When re-produced in everyday encounters, such discourses often emerged as attempts to situate Romanian nationals disadvantageously within particular settings.

> One of those guys at work, do you know what he said to me? He said, "It's all horses and carts over your way isn't it?" And he laughed. So, I replied. Do you know what I said to him? I said, "We are free to go and live anywhere in the EU. I chose to live in Paris and London. You chose to stay in [a small, market town in the North East of England]." He didn't respond to that! (Nelu, December 2014).

In this interaction, we see Nelu's colleague intersecting borderwork with boundary work by positioning Nelu within a particular hierarchisation of workers; migrants from Romania are situated as lower than others within the same workplace, based not solely on being 'from there' (borderwork), but because 'there' is economically deprived (classed boundary work). Nelu's colleague, like others, drew upon b/ordering discourses from popular media in referencing the poverty he has seen on news reports[4] covering the end of the transitional controls for Romanians and Bulgarians. Nelu's position was further undermined by state bordering, as unlike his colleagues, who were employed on permanent contracts with their employer, he was once again working for an agency. In his previous work in London, he had also been forced for a number of years to access work through an agency, because of the transitional controls. Through this 'false self-employment' (Ruhs and Wadsworth, 2018), he was paid less and received no holiday or sick pay for doing the same work as his colleagues.

Consequently, when he found himself subjected to this border-and-boundary work in his workplace in the North East, Nelu did not accept this positioning and contested it. This contestation (Reeves, 2014) illustrates that far from being carried unconsciously (Verhage, 2014), b/orders and boundaries are not only consciously noted by some members of minoritised groups, but are actively challenged; border-and-boundary work leads to the dialogical construction of b/orders and boundaries. Driven by his experiences of the intersections of structural inequalities emerging from state bordering and b/ordering discourses in the media, Nelu mocks the man for remaining in the small, deprived market town, and highlights that he has lived in two of Europe's global cities, clearly using his mobility to challenge the boundaries his colleagues seek to establish. For Nelu, immobility in a de-bordered EU situates his colleague below him. His colleague may belong in this small town, but Nelu asserts his belonging to a larger space – the European Union.

---

[4] Towards the end of 2013 and into 2014 when the transitional controls were removed, there was coverage in the UK media of some of the most impoverished communities in both Romania and Bulgaria (see Wemyss and Cassidy, 2017). This frequently included rural scenes with people travelling by horse-drawn cart.

I begin with Nelu's example specifically because he did not engage in the emotion work (Hochschild, 1993) that would enable the perpetuation of the b/ordered hierarchies and boundaries within the UK that his colleague sought to (re)produce. Yet, I came across many examples of situations in which Romanian nationals, when confronted with similar discourses, did not contest them as Nelu had done. Denisa, Nelu's older sister, encountered similar attitudes in her workplace, where Nelu had also worked for a period of time, but she did not engage in challenging the boundaries imposed upon her in the same way.

> Yes, everyone at work thinks we all live like those pictures they show of gypsies[5] in Romania. They think we have nothing (laughs). Seriously, my work colleagues think I live in some kind of shed. I don't tell them I have a house and land there. They think we are all living like gypsies. (Denisa, London, 2013)

Denisa's reference to 'all', shows that she understood these comments to be generalisable, i.e. about Romanians as a group, illustrating the ways in which this border-and-boundary work is both directed at an individual but at the same time pertains to and identifies a collective. Whilst Denisa did not directly contest this positioning of Romanians in the encounters within her workplace, she made it clear in the derisory tone with which she told the story that she did not accept this positioning. Whilst she may have observed the conventions that smoothed the 'intersubjective dance' (Verhage, 2014: 98) of the encounter, this was neither unconscious nor natural (ibid). Denisa was, in fact, employing emotion work, i.e. self-managing her emotions.

This use of emotion work was not novel for Denisa. She frequently engaged in emotion work within her home life. She had moved to London in 2009 after the birth of her first child in order to join her husband, whom she suspected of having an affair. Amongst other micro-aggressions in their domestic life, Denisa's husband frequently humiliated her in front of their son, who, as he grew, adopted his father's attitudes towards his mother. Denisa rarely contested this behaviour in the home; when her son called her stupid, it was the friend who spoke up to chastise the child. She never openly challenged this positioning of her as less than her husband, which reflected the patriarchal structures and boundary work to which she had been subjected since infancy. Denisa's everyday encounters at work and her (non)responses when subjected to border-and-boundary work can be understood as similarly shaped by emotion work.

Conclusion

At a time when we see a proliferation of formal or state borderwork in everyday encounters in the UK (Yuval-Davis et al., 2019), it is important that we analyse how underpinning b/ordering processes and practices and socio-cultural boundaries are shaping such work. Such analysis suggests a need to revisit a broader understanding of borderwork (Rumford, 2008; Reeves, 2014) that recognises the messiness of state spatiality as it is *worked out* in everyday life. In this article, I have illustrated that for Romanians living in the UK, borderwork performed by the majority population towards them can be better understood as an intersection of border-and-boundary work, through which they are excluded not only because they come from 'there', but because there is impoverished, somewhere economically deprived and therefore other. Whilst the borderwork described here may not be that of formal, state borderwork, through which residents determine the rights of others to access various key services and support, it often reflects and (re)produces the

---

[5] The reference to Roma is something I have explored elsewhere with my colleague Georgie Wemyss (Wemyss and Cassidy, 2017).

discourses that have emerged to justify everyday re-bordering in the UK (Wemyss and Cassidy, 2017).

The border-and-boundary work described is, at times, contested in everyday intersubjective encounters (Reeves, 2014). It has been my contention that in order to better understand why contestation emerges, we need to analyse everyday encounters through the lens of emotion work. In considering the examples of Denisa and Nelu, I suggest that *direct* contestation is less likely to emerge in the moment of the intersubjective encounter when an individual has grown accustomed to the self-management of their emotions, i.e. emotion work, in other settings. For Denisa, emotion work had become habitual in her home life and relationships with her immediate family. Therefore, I contend that it is the emotion work, which becomes unconscious (Kawale, 2004) and smooths the intersubjective encounter, rather than an acceptance of the imposed b/orders and boundaries (Verhage, 2014).

References

Anthias, F. and Yuval-Davis, N. (2005). Racialized boundaries: Race, nation, gender, colour and class and the anti-racist struggle. London and New York: Routledge.

Bartkowski, J. and Read, J. (2003). "Veiled submission: Gender, power, and identity among evangelical and Muslim women in the United States." Qualitative Sociology, 26(1): 71-92.

Cassidy, K. (forthcoming). "The Punitiveness of Everyday Bordering in the UK" in Sureau, T., Vojta, F. and Schlee, G. (eds.) On Punishment Berghahn: Oxford, New York.

Cassidy, K. (2018). "Everyday Bordering, Healthcare and the Politics of Belonging in Contemporary Britain" in Paasi A, Saarinen J, Zimmerbauer K and Prokkola E-K (eds.) Borderless worlds – for whom? Routledge: Abingdon, Oxon, pp.78-92.

Griffiths, M. (2017). "Foreign, criminal: a doubly damned modern British folk-devil" Citizenship Studies, 21(5): 527-546.

Hochschild, A.R. (1983). The Managed Heart: Commercialisation of Human Feeling, London: University of California Press.

Humphris, R. (2017). "Borders of home: Roma migrant mothers negotiating boundaries in home encounters", Journal of Ethnic and Migration Studies, 43(7): 1190-1204.

Kawale, R. (2004). "Inequalities of the heart: the performance of emotion work by lesbian and bisexual women in London, England". Social & Cultural Geography, 5(4): 565-581.

Navaro-Yashin, Y. (2002). The Faces of the State: Secularism and Public Life in Turkey. Princeton: Princeton University Press.

Potter, J.L. and Meier, I. (2020, January 10). Emotional Borderwork in the NHS [paper presentation]. Doctors within Borders Workshop, Lancaster, UK.

Reeves, M. (2014). Border Work: Spatial Lives of the State in Rural Central Asia Ithaca & London: Cornell University Press.

Ruhs, M. and Wadsworth, J. (2018). "The impact of acquiring unrestricted work authorisation on Romanian and Bulgarian migrants in the United Kingdom," ILR Review 71(4): 823-852.

Rumford, C. (2008). "Introduction: Citizens and Borderwork in Europe", Space and Polity, 12(1): 1-12.

Rumford, C. (2013). "Towards a Vernacularized Border Studies: The Case of Citizen Borderwork", Journal of Borderlands Studies, 28(2): 169-180.

van Houtum, H., Kramsch, O. T., and Zierhofer, W. (eds). (2005). B/ordering space. Aldershot: Ashgate.

van Houtum, H. and van Naerssen, T. (2002). "Bordering, ordering and othering". Tijdschrift voor economische en sociale geografie, 93(2): 125–36.

Vaughan-Williams, N. (2008). 'Borderwork beyond inside/outside? Frontex, the citizen-detective and the war on terror'. Space and Polity, 12(1): 63–79.

Verhage, F. (2014). "Living with(out) borders: the intimacy of oppression". Emotion. Space and Society, 11: 96-105.

Wemyss, G. and Cassidy, K. (2017). "People think that Romanians and Roma are the same": everyday bordering and the lifting of transitional controls. Ethnic and Racial Studies, 40(7): 1132-1150.

Yuval-Davis, N. (2013). 'A situated intersectional everyday approach to the study of bordering'. EUBORDERSCAPES, Working Paper no. 2. http://www.euborderscapes.eu/fileadmin/user_upload/Working_Papers/EUBORDERSCAPES_Working_Paper_2_Yuval-Davis.pdf.

Yuval-Davis, N. (2015). "Situated intersectionality and social inequality", Raisons politiques, (2): 91-100.

Yuval-Davis, N., Wemyss, G. and Cassidy, K. (2019). Bordering Cambridge: Polity Press.

Yuval-Davis, N., Wemyss, G. and Cassidy, K. (2018). "Everyday Bordering, Belonging and the Re- Orientation of British Immigration Legislation", Sociology, 52(2): 228-244.

July 2020
Volume: 17, **No**: 4, pp. 559 – 560
ISSN: 1741-8984
e-ISSN: 1741-8992
www.migrationletters.com

MIGRATION
LETTERS

Received: 14 May 2020
DOI: https://doi.org/10.33182/ml.v17i4.995

Parker, K. (2015). Making Foreigners: Immigration and Citizenship Law in America, 1600-2000. New York: Cambridge University Press. (xii + 259 pp., ISBN: 978-1-107-69851-2).

Reviewed by Stephanie Mae Pedron[1]

Making Foreigners by Professor Kunal Parker condenses four centuries of American immigration and citizenship policy to make a case for how Americans have historically rendered entire groups of people living both outside *and* inside of the U.S. as "foreign." Parker links the history of immigrants with that of women, political nonconformists, the poor, and persons of colour to develop new ways of comprehending what it means to be an outsider. Various scholars have referred to America as a 'gatekeeping nation' that excludes explicit groups of people. Parker brings a fresh perspective by combining a wide range of literature from several fields—immigration policy, citizenship law, and studies of race, gender, and the poor—to challenge readers to think differently about notions of belonging, subordination, and citizenship.

Citizenship is often viewed positively because it brings with it a sense of shared identity and the ability to participate in communal affairs, but Parker considers the acquisition of citizenship in a different light. He posits that it is the process of an outsider becoming *less* foreign (Parker, 2015: 12). Parker considers historical laws and landmark Supreme Court cases that show how, over time, different groups of people have been considered less like aliens due to shifting societal conceptions that altered the definition of what it means to be an outsider. Throughout his book, Parker shows how the subjection of foreigners is based on the false platform that they come from a far-off land. Parker claims that "a foreigner might come from across the ocean, from relatively nearby, or nowhere at all" (Parker, 2015: 25). Since the beginning, America's federal immigration laws had exclusionary aspects. For example, the 1790 Naturalization Act, which set the criteria for naturalization to free, white males of good moral character. Selective deployment of civil liberties and limited avenues for naturalization imposed a distinct kind of non-belonging to all of those that did not fit within the narrow mould outlined by the law. Although the 1790 Act is considered the first formal citizenship law, many restrictionist immigration controls preceded it. Parker emphasizes these within the first half of his book, which he dedicates to an exhaustive coverage of state-level immigration control activities during the Antebellum Period in America.

Parker demonstrates how restrictionist policies were not only used against those seeking to migrate into the country, but also against those already inside. In the beginning, the poor were designated as foreign due to Elizabethan poor laws that sought to regulate the poor by giving the town in which they were settled financial responsibility over them (Parker, 2015: 32). This resulted in mass exclusion of the poor and the adoption of practices that facilitated the influx of more "desirable" settlers. Following the Revolutionary War, the notion of citizenship, and subsequently the face of what was considered an outsider,·changed. In Chapter 4, in particular, Parker details the many exclusions that free blacks were subjected to such as their characterization as "occupants" or

[1] Stephanie Pedron, Georgia Southern University, United States. E-mail: pedronstephanie.sp@gmail.com.

"denizens"—rather than citizens—and the travel restrictions imposed upon them (Parker, 2015: 89). Parker also considers how women were excluded through the continuity of *baron* and *femme* laws, whereby a woman's legal rights, property, and status were subsumed by her husband upon marriage (Parker, 2015: 29). The Expatriation Act of 1907, for instance, stripped American women that married non-citizen men of their citizenship.

The second half of the book covers the Post-Civil War period. Parker outlines the rise of the federal immigration system and the emergence of novel forms of discrimination against different targets such as Asian-Americans due to the passage of the Chinese Exclusion Act in 1882. As the federal immigration structure grew, nationality-based immigration quotas were established and deportation was frequently used as a tool for social control—a tool that is still heavily applied to this day. Parker also covers the expansion of general grounds of exclusion to show how practices have evolved throughout the years. For a time, the most important reason for barring entry into the U.S. was based on whether the individual would become a public charge (Parker, 2015: 153).

In the book's coda, Parker reiterates his goal of redirecting the immigration conversation to consider the history of not only those coming from the territorial "outside," but also those already residing within (Parker, 2015: 221). Parker states that "the object of tracing this historical trajectory has been to reveal the manipulability of the border between citizen and alien" (Parker, 2015: 225). Based on this goal, *Making Foreigners* is a great success. Parker's coverage of so many groups over such an extended period does, however, cause him to glide over details that experts may wish for him to elaborate on. Furthermore, Parker's work would benefit from a review of immigration policy variations among the states during the Antebellum Period, particularly those with relatively friendlier immigration laws than what he described during his examination of the state of Massachusetts (Parker, 2015: 108). Nevertheless, Parker makes a compelling case against the enduring myth about America being a nation that has historically welcomed all immigrants.

For some, citizenship is little more than an option on a form; for others, it can shape their entire lives. Parker persuasively argues how public sentiment during a given time can have a profound impact on entire groups of people residing both inside and outside of America. *Making Foreigners* is a thoroughly researched work that challenges readers to rethink the conventional meaning of the word "foreigner" and re-examine historical instances when groups in the territorial 'inside' may have been subject to the same legal constraints as those typically considered non-citizens.

July 2020
Volume: 17, **No**: 4, pp. 561 – 562
ISSN: 1741-8984
e-ISSN: 1741-8992
www.migrationletters.com

MIGRATION
LETTERS

Received: 21 June 2020
DOI: https://doi.org/10.33182/ml.v17i4.1088

Schielke, Samuli. (2020). Migrant Dreams, Egyptian Workers in the Gulf States. Cairo: The American University in Cairo Press (xii + 154 pp., ISBN: 978-9-774169-56-4).

Reviewed by Rania M. Rafik Khalil[1]

Migrant Dreams is about the hopes and aspirations on which migrant workers thrive to achieve their goals. The first version of this book was published in 2017 in Arabic with the title *Hatta yantahi al-naft* (Until the End of Oil). Samuli Schielke explains that in order for him to understand Egypt, he needed to study the effects of international migration and foreign dependency. Based on over a decade of fieldwork, observations and conversations, Samuli Schielke gives a detailed overview of the life of low-income Egyptian migrant labourers who relocated to the Arab Gulf States on temporary contracts, returned, then migrated again. The book focuses mostly on the story of Tawfik, an intelligent Egyptian young man from rural backgrounds who is compelled to achieve the dream of marriage and building a family home, while in *ghurba* (away from home). The most important task of the book as Schielke puts it is "to describe how and under what conditions migrant workers live" (xv). He attempts to define the life of a migrant which is not really a life yet is entirely concerned with building a life.

Migrant Dreams engages with questioning the impact of migrating to the Gulf in relation to money, want of a better life, families, and communities back home. The narrow circle of life mostly revolves around the work site, accommodation provided by the contractor, buying food, calling home, and logging online. The author highlights the pros and cons of such a limited life overshadowed with the prospect of instant deportation of non-citizens. Labour migrants often experience subaltern racism which according to Schielke is not a coincidental side effect, but a functional part of the way countries in the Gulf are governed; "Subaltern racism is part of an architecture of power in which an entire society is systematically depoliticised and demobilised" (p.27). It reinforces the narrow circle of life, guiding workers' "dreams towards a specific circular path" (p.27). He highlights that the logic of separating "families" and "bachelors" is far more reaching than just separating unmarried men from families in public spaces and the poor from the rich but it is part of the system of segregating migrants into those who earn an income sufficient enough to send for their families to live with them and those who cannot afford the expenses to do so. Migrant work is a harsh reality, one that is often unsettling and alienating reduced to "making, saving and spending money" (p.44). Egyptian migrant labourers often want to appear successful in the eyes of their families and potential brides and consequently, they share very little about what they do and how they live. Ghurba, Schielke says "teaches one to suffer and to endure in pursuit of those inevitable dreams that can only be realised with the help of money" (p.57). Such a life makes it exceedingly difficult to pursue other dreams. The book interrupts the tracing of Tawif's life by commenting on the expulsion of thousands of migrant workers in 2013 and 2014 in the Gulf to replace them in the active workforce with citizens, and this coincided with the stagnation of the

---

[1] Dr Rania M. Rafik Khalil, The British University in Egypt (BUE), Egypt. E-Mail: rania.khalil@bue.edu.eg.

Egyptian economy. To tell a young Egyptian man at that time to forgo his dream of migrating to the Arab Gulf States, particularly those from villages, was equal to crushing his dreams. A paradoxical outcome of the pursuit of a better life through migratory labour is the difficulty of returning to the stable life one dreams to build back home. According to Schielke (2020), "Egypt is one of the many societies that rely heavily on migrants' remittances" (p.55). The chapter, Until the End of Oil points out that "the attempt to turn one's dreams into reality through migratory labour means, in practice, that one has to endure a less –than-real life while waiting for real life to begin. And one often has to do so over extended periods of time: for just one more year, until the end of oil" (p.78). Migrant money has, over the course of forty years, transformed some Egyptian villages into semi-urbanised communities with empty multi-story red brick buildings. Empowered by the economic gain accumulated in the Arab Gulf States, many who returned to Egypt perceived it with a "mixture of intimacy and estrangement" (p.87).

The author towards the second half of the book, points to the most debated issues according to his research and conversations with Tawfik and other migrant labours. Discussions revolved around "the impact that migration to the Gulf has on how Egyptians understand a good life in material, ethical, and spiritual terms" in addition to the how migration has often gone hand in hand with a deep conviction in destiny and a belief in God's unknown plans. He further points out that migration to the "Gulf has transformed Egypt's once pluralistic moderate and solidarity – oriented society into a religiously conservative intolerant and fiercely materialistic one" (p.92). Four pages later, however, he remarks that the Gulf is also "an important source of cosmopolitan, upper-class liberalism" (p.96).

Schielke shifts in the final chapters of his book to the notion of migrant money and the difficulties that must be endured away from home in order to make that home possible. He makes an attempt to tie the impact of migration labourers in villages in Egypt to a more global perspective by comparing it to the experience of migration for work in Finland and Sweden. It is not particularly a suitable approach from the perspective of an Egyptian reviewing the book. It weakened his argument and far from plausible. In his defence, though, the aim of this chapter The Shine of the Metropolis is to contextualise migration from rural areas to cities as being a world-wide phenomenon. The book ends with the final chapter concluding the argument that "migrants' initial aspirational dreams are not simply disappointed but rather transformed by experiences" (p.109).

Throughout the book, Samuli Schielke traces the endeavours of Tawfiq who helps Schielke in deepening his understanding of the dreams of Egyptian young men from rural areas and low-income families. Schielke depicts his dreams and struggles, resulting in a rich account of life as a migrant worker in the Gulf. *Migrant Dreams* is bound to appeal to international audiences as well as Middle East scholars interested in the detailed lives of labour migrants and their experiences.

www.ingramcontent.com/pod-product-compliance
Lightning Source LLC
Chambersburg PA
CBHW081741270326
41932CB00020B/3357